# Coping With Stepfamilies

# Coping With Stepfamilies

by
Leslie S. Kaplan

THE ROSEN PUBLISHING GROUP
New York

Published in 1986, 1988, 1991 by The Rosen Publishing Group, Inc.
29 East 21st Street, New York, NY 10010

Copyright © 1986, 1988, 1991 by Leslie S. Kaplan

All rights reserved. No part of this publication may be reproduced in any form without permission in writing from the publisher, except by a reviewer.

**Revised Edition 1991**

**Library of Congress Cataloging in Publication Data**
Kaplan, Leslie S. (Leslie Schenkman)
 Coping with stepfamilies.

 1. Stepfamilies—United States.  2. Stepchildren—United States—Family relationships.  3. Young adults—United States—Family relationships.  4. Family—United States.  I. Title

HQ759.92.K37   1985      646.7'8      85-14245
ISBN 0-8239-1371-1

*Manufactured in the United States of America.*

## *Acknowledgments*

Many people helped make *Coping with Stepfamilies* accurate, interesting, and readable. I sincerely thank Mayer and Susan Levy and Joan Dawson for their painstaking, in-depth review of the manuscript and their very useful comments. Every conversation with them led to valuable additions to the text. Sallye Petruchyk and Susan Piland assisted with their incisive remarks, pet peeves, and vivid anecdotes based on their extensive professional and personal experiences. Don and Page Roberts' detailed editorial suggestions helped make the book easier to read. Special thanks also go to Jerry Schenkman, Ken and Maggie Bowen, Allen Salken, and Bill Brockman for sharing their ideas.

Most important, these persons added the strong belief that stepfamily life can be a positive and satisfying experience. While the literature takes a pessimistic view of stepfamilies, they remind us that not all stepfamilies have problems, although they all do have adjustments. Stepfamilies do not cause difficulties; people do. And many, many people do not.

For their help and encouragement—as well as to all the parents and young people who shared the personal aspects of their lives in stepfamilies—I express my deepest appreciation.

A very special thank you to Michael Kaplan for arranging his schedule so that I could prepare this book on mine.

## About the Author

Leslie Schenkman Kaplan, EdD, is Director of Guidance for the York County, Virginia, Public Schools. She is a Licensed Professional Counselor and a National Board Certified Counselor who works primarily with adolescents. She knows young people through her active involvement as a high school and middle school guidance counselor, a peer counselor trainer, a hotline consultant, and a private practitoner. Dr. Kaplan's articles on dealing with adolescents appear in national educational and counseling journals, and she gives presentations on these topics at state and national meetings. She also teaches graduate counseling and education courses at The College of William and Mary in Williamsburg, Virginia.

Dr. Kaplan earned a BA degree in English from Rutgers University, an MA from Columbia University, an MS in Counseling from the University of Nebraska at Omaha, and a doctorate from The College of William and Mary.

Dr. Kaplan serves as an Independent Examiner from the Virginia Board of Professional Counselors and on editorial boards for *The School Counselor* and the *Virginia Counselors Association Journal*. She was named Virginia Counselor of the Year, 1988.

Dr. Kaplan currently lives in Newport News with her husband, Dr. Michael L. Kaplan, a research meteorologist, and their son, Reid.

## Contents

|  | Introduction | ii |
|---|---|---|
| I. | When One Parent Dies | 1 |
| II. | The Divorce Experience | 13 |
| III. | Living in a Single-Parent Family | 34 |
| IV. | Becoming a Stepfamily | 53 |
| V. | Living with a Stepparent | 84 |
| VI. | Living with a Stepbrothers and Stepsisters | 105 |
| VII. | Adolescents in Stepfamilies | 121 |
| VIII. | A Troubled Stepfamily | 146 |
| IX. | When One Parent is Gay | 155 |
| X. | Coping with Stepfamilies | 160 |
|  | Bibliography | 175 |
|  | Index | 179 |

# Introduction

The biggest problem facing stepfamilies is a poor public image.

The first problem stepfamilies face is the name, "stepfamily." This is not a positive, upbeat term. "Step-" anything means "orphaned" or "bereaved." It means "a step away" from the real thing. It suggests that a stepfamily is not a real family. "Step-" is second-best, just as Cinderella, Snow White, and Hansel and Gretel were mistreated stepchildren. By tradition, stepmothers are "wicked." Absent fathers are "Disneyland Dads" who entertain—but do not raise—their children on weekends or holidays.

People try to give stepfamilies a better image by using terms such as "blended" or "reconstituted" family. Whatever the name, stepfamily still suggests not good enough.

When people think of stepfamilies, they think of failure. Stepfamilies are built on loss. A stepfamily comes together when one parent remarries after a divorce or a death. Stepchildren either have experienced one parent's death or have an absent parent living somewhere else. At least one adult in a stepfamily is bravely trying marriage again.

Stepparents are expected to act like parents, to set and enforce family rules, to support the household, to be involved in family activities; but a stepparent lacks the love and importance possessed by their stepchildren's natural parent. The losses that lead to stepfamilies are part of the poor public image.

When people think of a stepfamily, they become confused about who belongs. Most people think that a "family" is two parents living together with one or more of their natural children in one home. When they lock the front door at night and go to sleep, everyone who belongs in the family is there.

On the other hand, many stepfamilies have absent parents, absent children, and many sets of aunts, uncles, cousins, and grandparents. Mothers have last names different from their children's. Stepfamilies have children living as brother and sister who are not related, except that one of their parents is married to the other's parent. Two married adults and one or more children live together in a home, but one of each child's natural parents lives somewhere else. A stepfamily may be a family in which one or both married adults has a child or children from an earlier marriage who lives with the ex-wife or ex-husband and whom the child visits from time to time. A stepfamily is a family in which someone who belongs to one family member lives in another place, and so children feel as if they "belong" in both homes. The situation sometimes becomes so confusing that stepchildren feel as if they belong nowhere.

Stepfamilies look like families, but they don't feel like first families. They may feel like strangers to one another. One of the adults has had a longer relationship with one of the children than with the other adult. When an argument starts between stepparent and stepchild, the natural parent is torn between supporting the new spouse and supporting his or her own child. Stepparent and child are thrown together through marriage without the slow growth of love and caring that comes from giving birth and feeding and nurturing over many years. Stepfamily members are expected to love each other, but they hardly know each other and may not even like each other. In fact, stepchildren bitterly resent a stepparent who tries to act as a replacement for their absent parent. Stepchildren feel strong loyalty and love for their absent parent, and they worry that liking or cooperating with a stepparent means that they have stopped loving their absent natural parent. If stepparents have natural children who live elsewhere, they often feel the same way about their stepchildren.

Whatever the problems, stepfamilies are real families, and their numbers are growing. Thirty-five million adults and seven million children in the United States live in stepfamilies. One out of every five children under age eighteen lives in a stepfamily. About 1,300 new stepfamilies are formed each day. One third of all American children do not live in a traditional mother-father-in-the-same-house family. One half of all marriages are remarriages for one of the adults. According to the 1980 U.S. Census, 75 percent of all marriages are first marriages, 20 percent of all marriages are second marriages, and 6 percent are third marriages. Of the 1,300 couples who form stepfamilies each day, 60 percent will probably divorce. By the year 2000 the stepfamily may be the most common form of family in the United States. The trend for the stepfamily seems clear.

What is not clear, however, are the rules for becoming a happy, successful stepfamily. When people believe that the only real family is the "first-family" model and the only real family rules are first-family rules, they make problems for themselves in their second family. The first-family model does not fit stepfamilies. And it does not have to fit. Stepfamilies *are real families*. They are not first families, and they do not have to be.

Stepfamily members do not have to love one another in order to be happy or to be a real family. Stepparents do not have to be replacement parents to their stepchildren in order to have a happy real family. Stepchildren can keep on loving their absent parent, whether dead or living across town, and still appreciate and like their stepparents without being disloyal. Stepfamilies do not have to force the togetherness first-family model on their own activities. Stepfamilies can allow for individual differences. Not everyone who belongs in the family has to live under the same roof in order to be a real family.

Stepfamilies are real families. Becoming a new family takes longer than the marriage ceremony. It takes time, shared experiences, open minds, patience, goodwill, flexible rules, and the true desire to build honest, caring relationships for stepfamilies to become healthy and happy places to live for adults and children.

# Coping With Stepfamilies

# CHAPTER I

## *When One Parent Dies*

Stepfamilies come together in many ways. A single parent marries for the first or second time; the new husband or wife becomes the children's stepparent. A parent in another family dies; the children and surviving parent live awhile as a single-parent family. Eventually the surviving parent remarries. The new mate becomes a stepparent. Sometimes children living with a single parent watch their absent parent remarry. These children gain a stepparent whom they occasionally visit but with whom they do not live. In all these instances, intimate emotional and biological relationships between children and their parent exist before the relationship between the parent and new spouse begins.

Before a stepfamily begins, a first family comes apart. Divorce or death brings tremendous conflict, confusion, and sadness to a family. Nothing seems as it was, and the whole world is wrenched inside out. Parents suffer and children suffer. Before the tragedy, family members go about their day-to-day lives expecting things to go on forever as usual. They plan their activities, set their goals, and dream their dreams around the "givens" of having a mother, father, and home always there for them. People want life to continue as they know it, and few adults or children dare think about living in any other way. When the breakup comes, they experience shock and pain unlike anything they ever felt before.

While both death and divorce lead to major changes in a family, children and adults sometimes experience the two events in different ways. The events themselves and the ways family members respond to them strongly impact the success of any future stepfamily.

### *Losing a Parent through Death*

Living with caring parents teaches children a most important lesson: how to love and be loved. People depend on love continuing, believing that if they love, love will be returned. They trust relationships to go on despite illness, arguments, and small separations. People count on their parents and spouse being there to give advice, guidance, protection, and love.

But the unthinkable happens. Sudden accidents explode without warning and parents die. Serious illnesses arise, and parents die. Old age wears down the body and physical decline ends in death. One day a complete family sits down to dinner, and the next day all but one dress in mourning black.

Children respond to death in a number of ways. The child's age affects the way young people react. Very young children are not able to imagine what death is. They do not really understand death's finality, and they are confused about whether or not the deceased parent will return. Cartoon characters they see on TV regularly fall from high cliffs, are hit by cars, or are chopped into small pieces, yet they always return intact and healthy in the next frame. Young children under age five often think that death means going away for awhile, and children that young wait for their dead parent's return. In addition, these children understand only what they can see and touch. In their mind, a person who has died retains all the qualities of a person who is alive; a dead person may be in a box or in the sky eating, drinking, playing cards, or folding laundry. The deceased parent does what the children typically remember him or her doing while alive.

Children aged five to ten understand what adults tell them about death and know that it is a final, lasting separation. From age eleven onward, children more fully understand death as adults do. As a result of these differences in understanding, children of varying ages respond to news of a parent's death in different ways.

The type of relationship the children and their deceased parent shared also influences the ways children respond to the death. Younger children depend on their parent's protection and care. When the idea of death's finality sinks in, they experience terror along with grief. They wonder, fearfully, "Who will take care of me now?"

Children who experienced a close and loving relationship with their parent feel the loss with tremendous grief. Even children who fought bitterly and often with the parent shared an intense closeness. Their pain of loss mixes with their guilty thoughts about having somehow added to the death by creating extra stress for the deceased parent. They feel guilty for having wished in angry moments for the parent to go away. These children know in their mind that thoughts cannot kill, but they still feel at fault and hate themselves for the way they treated their parent. For them grieving takes longer, because they must forgive themselves before they can successfully mourn for their deceased parent and before they can feel ready to like a stepparent.

Older children who have already begun leading separate and independent lives also feel deep grief and loss. They do not, however, have the fear of dependent youngsters or the guilt of those children who had angrily argued with their parent before the death. Preteens and adolescents are able to deal in effective and self-sufficient ways in the world. Older children also have more outside support for their grief; they can share their sadness and anger with helpful friends, teachers, and relatives.

Children of different ages respond to a parent's death in different ways. Fred, age fifteen, looked at his mother's picture on his desk and sat down to think. He could not believe she was dead. Just last week, she had taken him shopping for new running shoes and socks for his next track meet. Fred had acted calm at the funeral but had cried plenty in the privacy of his room afterwards. He kept thinking about his mother, the accident, and the times they had shared together. He thought about her all the time and saw her face in his mind a million times a day. Meanwhile he went to school, did his work, and tried to help Dad with the two little kids.

Jeremy, age four, seemed okay. Jeremy said Mom was in heaven, cooking dinners for the angels and giving baths to all the little children who had died. What nonsense, thought Fred, but at least Jeremy was not acting as bratty as Sheila. She was nine and behaving like a colossal pain in the neck. She was constantly arguing with him over nothing, starting fights with Dad, and teasing Jeremy. She was asking to be clobbered. She acted mean and selfish, just as she used to act with Mom. Dad did not need the extra hassles now. Sheila did not help set the table or pick up her clothes as she used to. Fred was fed up. Didn't Sheila know she was making matters worse with all her fussing?

Circumstances surrounding a parent's death also influence how children respond to the death. People cannot prepare themselves for sudden accidents. The shock, denial, and anger at the unfairness and senselessness of unnecessary death keep family members grieving longer because accepting the reality is so hard.

On the other hand, mourning for a parent who dies after a long and terrible illness such as cancer or heart disease is not easy, either. One might expect that knowing ahead of time of a parent's dying allows family members to become used to the idea and begin letting go emotionally during the illness, but that does not always happen. The reverse may be true, and those persons who care daily for the ill parent actually become more involved and more attached through the continual day-to-day contacts. Although death may come as a relief from pain and suffering for the sick person as well as for family members, the death at last is still a time of sadness.

The parent's sex is another factor affecting how children respond to the death. Children learn to accept their identity as male or female by watching adult models in their lives. Boys identify with their father's behavior and say to themselves, "I am a man and that is how men are supposed to act." Girls say similar things about their mother. Children also learn how to be men or women by interacting with the parent of the opposite sex. They learn how women behave with men and how men behave with women. These lessons take years of involvement. When a parent dies when children are young, much about becoming comfortable as men or women remains unlearned. Children confused about who they are sometimes act in strange ways, behaving as they imagine men or women are supposed to behave. A young boy whose father dies might start acting bossy, rude, and uncooperative at home, imagining that real men act tough and independent. A young girl whose mother dies might start acting possessive and overprotective toward younger brothers and sisters or become a perfect little homemaker, thinking that real women are supposed to act in these ways. Both children give stepparents difficult times with these mistaken ideas. For example, boys resist their stepfather's discipline and limit-setting, and girls resent their stepmother's taking over the important jobs they had in their single-parent family.

A final factor influencing the way children respond to a parent's death is the surviving parent's ability to provide a supportive climate for successful mourning. Children feel loss deeply and need time and chances to grieve. They need occasions to feel sad about never seeing their dead parent again. They need chances to be angry about their parent's leaving them. Children need time to be angry with themselves for adding to the dead parent's burdens or for not lessening the parent's pain. Children wonder whether the deceased parent really loved them. It is best to keep memories of the deceased parent alive, while at the same time giving up the departed as an object of love. In this way, grieving persons can one day feel free to love again.

Mourning is not easy for persons feeling loss or for those nearby. No one enjoys hearing another person cry. No one likes seeing another person so sad that he or she cannot eat, sleep, play, or have fun anymore. Hearing children express natural, honest sadness or anger about a dead parent upsets the surviving parent. A parent wants children to be happy again and to let the past be over so that all can move ahead with their lives. Nevertheless, the children's feelings of grief are real, and children need to feel, hear, and understand their pain for it to finally end. Children's grieving behavior is necessary if they are to accept the loss and feel free to love others.

Sandy, for instance, was not allowed to mourn for her father. She felt so tight she thought she would shatter, she missed her Dad so much. Even having known of his serious illness for weeks did not prepare her for his death. He had promised to build her a large doll house, and he had piled the lumber along the garage wall ready to begin. Every time she went outside to get her bike, she saw the wood and cried.

Mother was a wreck. Screaming and crying was all Sandy heard. At other times, Mother sat and stared out the kitchen window for hours. She did not even bother to dress some days. When Sandy tried to comfort her and talk about Dad's death, Mother turned away or told her to shut up. If Sandy looked sad, Mother would tell her to stop moping. If Sandy forced a smile and tried to act cheerful to help Mother feel better, Mother would yell that Sandy did not care at all about her Dad.

Sandy felt she could not win. Nothing she said or did was right. When Mother cleared Dad's clothes out of the bedroom closet and gave them to the Salvation Army, Sandy freaked. How could

Mother do that? Sandy felt lonelier than ever before in her whole life. She did not want to burden her friends with her troubles, and Mother did not want to hear them, either. So Sandy thought about her Dad all the time by herself, careful not to upset her Mother anymore. She no longer thought about friends or fun, or school. She just became sadder and lonelier.

Surviving parents and older children need to understand the grieving process so as not to allow their own discomfort and loss to interfere with their children's natural mourning process. For a parent to say, "Don't say such mean things about your father. He's dead!" forces children to feel guilty about their natural and genuine emotions and forces young people to shut off the process of accepting and letting go before they are ready to do so. For a parent to say, "You don't seem to care" to silently grieving children makes the young people feel as if they are bad persons for not loving their dead parent enough. These responses from a parent make mourning and letting go harder.

When children are scolded for their grief-caused sadness or anger, their real emotions go underground. Children act the way they think their parents want them to act. If punished for expressing real but uncomfortable feelings, children bury those feelings. If a surviving parent wants cheerful children, children will put on upbeat behaviors. If children think parents want to forget their own sadness, they act well behaved, gay, and cheerful, denying what they really feel inside. When children cover up their emotions often enough and hard enough, they forget what it means to feel at all. In such cases, they will not allow themselves to feel close to a stepparent or to risk the hurt of loss again.

Children need time and chances to experience loss of a parent in their own ways. Crucial outcomes depend on their doing so. First, death shatters children's trust in relationships. They totally trusted their parent always to be available for love and safety. Death was a betrayal. Does this mean they should never let themselves feel close to another person again? If people risk caring deeply for others, will they feel this terrible pain of loss in the future? Successful grieving means feeling the sadness, anger, and depression that come before acceptance of loss and ability to love in the future.

Children not permitted to experience their feelings about loss start idealizing their dead parent. Not allowed to feel pain, children are also not free to remember the whole person with strengths and faults. If a dead parent becomes "the most wonderful parent that ever was," no live flesh-and-blood adult will be able to measure up to the fantasy image. A stepparent does not stand a chance of being accepted as caring, helpful, or likable.

Permission to feel bad or sad or angry comes from watching the surviving parent successfully grieve and from the surviving parent's understanding and acceptance of the children's pain. The relationship between children and their surviving parent depends on the outcome. The relationship between children and any future stepparent does, too.

*When Widowed Parents Remarry*

Does the death of one parent in a family make it easier or harder for all involved when the surviving parent remarries? Professionals disagree about the answer. Adjustment to a stepfamily after one parent's death still depends on the persons involved and the situation in which they find themselves. Remarriages after widowhood, however, do have a lower divorce rate than do first marriages.

Surviving parents love their children now more than ever. The beloved spouse and parent is gone. The surviving parent and children lean heavily on each other after the crisis for comfort, understanding, and shared grief. They need each other's help to keep the household running. The parent takes on new cooking and carpool duties. Children begin picking up after themselves and tending to laundry and cleanup chores. The family members greatly depend on pulling together to make the family work, and they come through the difficult days feeling increased appreciation, closeness, and respect for each other.

Yet the surviving parent often feels lonely for the company of other adults. With emotional supports gone, the parent does not want to burden children with the adult's emotional and social ups and downs. A single parent no longer comes home and talks about frustrations, fears, and dreams with a loving spouse. His or her sex life has also ended, and a parent misses the intimate sharing, tenderness, and physical pleasure experienced between two loving adults.

The shared routines of Sunday's three-hour breakfasts and dining in favorite restaurants have ended. A parent misses the feeling of solidarity that comes from solving problems together and working toward common goals. Many parents accept the loneliness and go on as single parents. Some choose escape through tranquilizers, by denial of sad feelings, or by deliberately forgetting. In any case, many surviving parents decide to alter the loneliness through remarriage.

Certain things do make remarriage after widowhood an easier adjustment than after divorce. For one thing, society respects widowhood more than divorce. When a parent dies, no one is blamed. No one has failed at marriage or parenthood. A surviving parent has the community's condolences, support, and best wishes for future happiness. A surviving parent has positive social standing and nothing about which to feel embarrassed, ashamed, or guilty. Thus he or she does not feel the internal pressures to make up for past mistakes by rushing into a new marriage with the goal of making everything right this time. A widowed parent does not need to regain a feeling of self-worth through remarriage as does many a divorced parent who feels a failure at marriage. Neither does the surviving parent feel outside pressure to escape from an uncomfortable social position by rushing into a new marriage.

In addition, widowed parents are usually older than divorced parents, and their children are also older. As a result, surviving parents feel little need to seek a "substitute parent" for young children. Then, too, grieving takes much time to resolve well. Unlike parents who were unhappy with each other's company and wanted to end the relationship through divorce, a widowed parent usually enjoyed a satisfying relationship with the late spouse until death interfered. Therefore, a widowed parent needs more time to mourn than does a divorced parent. Moreover, many a widowed parent experiences less desire to remarry at all. The first marriage was so satisfying that it seems doubtful whether the positive experience could be repeated in a second marriage. Not wanting to settle for less, this parent may decide to remain single. All in all, if remarriage occurs after one parent dies, it has many things in its favor.

On the other hand, many things in widowhood suggest difficult problems for a stepfamily coming together in remarriage. For one thing, although the children's Mom or Dad and the surviving parent's husband or wife has died, the children and surviving parent still have relationships with the deceased person, who was a much loved mother, father, husband, or wife. Simply because the parent or spouse no longer physically lives does not mean he or she is not present in the survivors' thoughts. Problems arise when a stepparent or surviving parent views the new spouse as a "replacement parent" rather than an additional parent. Children bitterly resent any stepparent's trying to take their natural parent's place.

When a natural parent is dead, a stepparent is more likely to assume the replacement role in attitude and behavior. Stan became a stepfather with the highest intentions. He was going to be the best Dad those two boys could ever hope for. The poor kids' natural father was ill for so long that he could not do much for them. Now Stan would take the ten-year-old to ball games and teach him to play soccer and tennis. He had already bought circus tickets for the five-year-old the next weekend. Stan was kind, friendly, youthful, and enthusiastic about his new family, but he was also puzzled by the boys' coldness toward him. They were polite, of course. Their mother had raised them to be well-mannered gentlemen. Yet they always had excuses for not wanting to do things with him, or if they went along, they seemed quiet and bored. Stan would be patient and try a little harder. He did not understand why the boys kept their Dad's picture on their dresser when Stan was right there in the flesh to help them and give them a good time. Stan did not realize that memories keep important others very much alive and present in stepchildren's thoughts.

Sadly, while children keep emotional ties with their deceased parent, they have nowhere to turn if the situation with a stepparent becomes difficult. If they have lost a parent through divorce, children have both emotional links and a real physical person and place to which to turn when they feel the desire to leave home. Children of a deceased parent cannot pack up and live with Mom or Dad when the problems at home become too stressful. Instead, they have the emotional bonds tying them to other, unavailable persons but few practical choices from which to act.

Emotional ties to a dead parent bring "ghosts" into stepfamilies. A surviving parent and children remember how the first parent acted. They remember how she prepared delicious meals, how he could fix anything broken, how clean and attractive the children and home looked, and what fine times they had together. Whether real in fact or real in imagination, a stepparent has to deal with memories of the deceased parent whom no one wanted to leave and whom everyone still misses. Unlike divorce where adults deliberately choose to separate, a stepparent in a widowed family lives with constant critical comparisons. Reminders of the deceased parent become a threat or a rival to the new spouse. No one feels confident when continually compared to idealized persons who live only in others' memories. In a stepfamily, no one wins this imaginary but very real competition.

In addition, both the surviving parent and children sometimes feel guilty about the remarriage. It becomes a betrayal of a departed loved one who did not willingly leave the family. The surviving parent sometimes finds that looking at the children is a reminder of the lost spouse and brings a feeling of being disloyal and unfaithful either to the children or to the deceased. The surviving parent feels guilty and ashamed of the natural desire to move forward with life and feel free to enter new relationships. What is more, children feel guilty if they begin to like and appreciate their new stepparent; they suspect that affection for a stepparent is disloyal to the dead parent.

Children feel anger toward a new stepparent on other counts. If the children had taken on many household jobs after their parent's death, they now resent their stepparent's shoving them aside by taking on the adult roles the youngsters once filled. They feel less valued, less important, and less appreciated even as they enjoy relief from the added chores. They feel pushed out of the special relationship they shared with their surviving parent. Children often believe their stepparent unfairly takes what rightly belongs to others, namely, a special place in their family. They bitterly resent a stepparent's entering the family and getting all the love, care, and attention that only the natural parent and children deserve.

*Is Death or Divorce Harder on Stepfamilies?*

Death comes without welcome. A parent does not want to die. A parent truly loves the spouse and children. No parent wants to make life unhappy for the family. Unfortunately, this choice is not his or hers to make.

A surviving parent and children face tragic losses together and go on with their lives the best they can.

A family of divorce experiences loss, too, but with a difference. Divorce means the marriage was unhappy for at least one partner. The adults separated by choice. The ex-spouse remains alive and living elsewhere. While adults can become ex-spouses, they cannot become ex-parents. Parents in divorce can still retain active and meaningful ties with their children, even if not on a daily basis.

The issue of choice has important consequences for the stepfamily. In a divorce, a parent frequently feels like a failure and brings bruised feelings about self-worth into remarriage. A divorced parent feels the need to prove his or her value and competence as a spouse and as a parent. In addition, a divorced parent feels guilty about having caused the children so much turmoil and suffering and wants to make up for past hurts. A divorced parent also experiences anger toward the former spouse. As a result, a divorced adult brings much unfinished business into remarriage, and this generates stress for all members in a stepfamily.

Death brings a different situation. A family has lost a vital member through no choice or decision by anyone. Most often, the adults shared a satisfying marriage and the surviving parent feels competent and valuable as a spouse and as a parent. He or she has nothing to prove to self or others by remarrying. If he or she decides to marry again, it is done from a background of success. A surviving parent has time, patience, and desire to make the best choice about a future mate.

For children, however, remarriage after one parent's death still brings difficulties. Young people resent a new adult's trying to take the place of their natural parent. They feel angry with the surviving parent for betraying the deceased parent by remarrying. Fortunately, children in this situation have positive attitudes about themselves. They soon realize that their deceased parent did not choose to leave them. They see themselves as lovable and valuable persons. After grieving ends, they know that relationships can be trusted and dependable. As a result, they may be more willing to adjust to a stepfamily if their surviving parent and the new stepparent let them keep emotional ties to the deceased parent through pleasant memories and allow them time and opportunity to grieve. When squabbles arise at home, children whose parent died argue with a stepparent just as they did with the natural parent, but they eventually work things out. These children cannot bluster and threaten to pack their bags and live with the other parent, so they stay home and solve their problems. Remarriage after one parent dies has a good chance of becoming a satisfying stepfamily.

*Conclusion*

Grief is personal. Not everyone feels and shows loss the same way. The sadness, anger, and depression are real feelings. They are natural feelings to have after someone you love dies.

Many children and adults are afraid to show their true emotions to others in the family because they don't want to make the survivors feel even worse. They hold back the unpleasant thoughts and feelings from relatives and friends so as not to remind them of the pain they all share. Sometimes people even keep these sad emotions and thoughts from themselves. They keep busy doing things that focus their attention away from the things that really matter.

Yet all these emotions must be felt, understood, and constructively expressed if the people feeling them are to get on with their lives. Surviving parents, children, and other relatives and friends must feel and talk out the sadness, discuss their shared memories, and remember the special times they had with their loved one. They need to note the uniqueness of the person they all miss and recall the ways that person cared about them. The person who died had good points and bad points, and it helps families to remember the whole person, faults and all. Remembering a dead loved one's failings does not mean one loved that person less. It means one accepts that real person more.

Of course tears will come. Laughter, too, will come, with a shared sense of togetherness. Finally, fully experiencing and expressing loss brings peace of mind and the ability, while never forgetting, to move on with their lives.

Stepparents must encourage or at least allow this remembering and sharing without feeling threatened. Children and adults must grieve for loved ones if they are ever to have the emotions open to love the stepparent.

# CHAPTER II

## *The Divorce Experience*

In earlier years, most stepfamilies formed after one parent died. The economic hardships of the times almost required two adults at home, one earning money or goods for basic needs, and the other raising the children and running the household. In addition, until 1957 most divorces occurred between couples without children. Youngsters at home kept unhappy couples together "for the children's sake." Parents either waited until youngsters grew up and became self-sufficient before divorcing or sacrificed their personal needs to keep the family together.

Today, children do not prevent or postpone their parents' divorce. In 1980, 100 out of every 1,000 couples in the U.S. divorced, half of them with children under eighteen.

The decision whether or not to divorce considers two points of view. In earlier times, parents believed that divorce "scarred children for life" by destroying the feeling of security that comes with family living. Children needed to be able to trust in ongoing family relationships or they would never be able to trust themselves or others. Believing this, parents postponed or gave up divorce. Many experts still hold this idea, saying that parents should remain together unless the household is so bitter or violent that children and adults both risk physical or emotional harm from living together.

A large number of parents and professionals today believe the reverse. They say children are hurt more by living in families whose members constantly fight. They believe that watching daily put-downs and cruelties between angry parents harms children's image of themselves and impairs their ability to one day develop their own satisfying relationships.

Parents must decide for themselves which of these two arguments carries more weight for them.

## 14 COPING WITH STEPFAMILIES

*Why Parents Divorce*

Parents divorce for any number of reasons. Every divorce differs. What makes a forceful reason to divorce in one family is only an inconvenience to live with in another. The list of causes for divorce is as long and as unique as the particular family:

"Your Mom shows no interest, concern, or affection for me anymore."

"I cannot trust your Dad anymore because of his lying, drinking, gambling, staying out late."

"Your Mom doesn't love me anymore; she loves someone else."

"Your Dad beats me, and I will no longer take his insults and abuse."

"Your Mom is mentally ill and treats you children cruelly and unfairly. She does not recognize her problem and will not get help to correct it."

"Although I love you children very much, my marriage is simply not working. I have important needs that this marriage cannot meet, and I want the chance to find happiness elsewhere."

The list goes on and on. Some families share closeness. They spend time together in activities such as camping, vacationing at the beach, attending church, and celebrating special occasions. Other families share only anger and physical violence.

Homes filled with open or hidden tensions cause stress for all family members. Children fear that their parents will seriously hurt each other. Young people refuse to bring friends home lest they witness a blowup between battling parents. In other homes the mood is so tense that everyone feels uptight trying to avoid disturbing the uneasy calm. Younger children respond to this home climate with physical ailments, vomiting, nervous tics, or weight loss because they never feel hungry enough to eat. Older children stay away from home as much as possible, remaining late at school or visiting friends. Everyone senses the tension, but no one dares say it aloud. They are afraid they will start something terrible that will not stop until the family shatters.

In still other homes, children are not aware of their parents' conflicts. Marital stresses do not always enter into relationships between parents and children. Occasionally, mothers or fathers build especially satisfying bonds with their children in attempts to balance their unhappiness with their spouse. In fact, parents may agree on child-raising issues but strongly disagree about many other important concerns. As a result, children sometimes are happy and content in spite of their parents' sufferings.

Most important, most children believe their home is a happy place before the divorce. They may not know about their parents' pain. Their parents protect them by not talking about marital problems or by not expressing personal sadness in front of them. Children do not have enough experience to recognize problems between their parents. Their family seems normal. Used to their parents' fights, children do not see the strain.

Other children see what they want to see and deliberately ignore the tensions around them. The idea that parents might have serious problems is too scary even to think about. These young people pretend their parents are happy. They do not think about what it means when one parent moves out of the bedroom and sleeps in the den. They turn their backs when parents begin drinking liquor too often. They pretend not to notice the silences between their parents or the absence of the affection the adults used to share.

Even when children know or suspect that their parents are unhappy, most prefer to keep them together rather than face divorce. To many children, parents are not real people, anyway. Parents fix meals, keep house, hand out spending money, make and enforce rules. Until adolescence, children have difficulty identifying with their parents as real people with special needs and interests, strengths and weaknesses, who might wish to leave an unhappy marriage.

Other children who can understand the reasons for divorce with their head cannot understand them in their heart. They still wish their parents could stay together, and they wonder hopelessly why the adults cannot make everything right again.

Divorce shocks and upsets most children, whether or not they suspected it might be coming. It hurts to hear the word "divorce," and it hurts to live with unhappy, angry parents. In certain cases, however, this is not true. Children may react to their parents' divorce with relief and thankfulness in instances where they have been beaten, tortured, or continually threatened with bodily harm.

Older children and adolescents sometimes view divorce as a relief if they have known of their parents' long-term suffering.

Wendy was glad it was finally over. She picked up her books and walked to the corner to meet her friends for the ride to school. She could not believe she was not more upset about the news. Her mother and father had sat down with the three kids last night and told them they were divorcing. Dad had already found an apartment and was moving tonight. The little ones cried and asked their folks to change their minds, but not Wendy. Wendy was tired of the arguments, tired of cleaning up the broken dishes after her parents' fights, tired of hearing Mom crying and complaining about the bruises Dad's beatings left on her. Wendy was tired of being scared all the time that one day Dad would become really violent with Mom, herself, or one of the little ones.

When her friend Debbie's parents had split up last year, Debbie had cried for weeks. She missed her Dad a lot and never thought her parents' problems were so big they could not be fixed. Every family has arguments; that is normal. Why should argument spell divorce?

Wendy wondered what to tell Debbie and the rest about her family's situation, asking herself if something was wrong with her for not feeling sad. What Wendy really felt, deep down, was glad and relieved that she could finally get on with her own life without the worry and fear at home.

*Children Need to Know More About the Divorce*

Parents usually know divorce is coming long before their children do. Parents feel emotionally and physically drained by constant conflict. Making the decision to separate brings added stress. Mothers and fathers worry that their children will be upset, unhappy, angry, and frightened at the news.

The parents are right. Most children meet the news with tears and beg their parents to change their minds. Some children offer bribes of gifts or good behavior in efforts to persuade them to change their plans. Some children feel panic and fear about what will happen to them if their family separates. Will they have to move away from their home, school, and friends? Will they have to say goodbye to one parent? Other children experience tremendous anger toward their parents. A few children hear the news and sit in stunned silence, unable to move or react at all. They walk aimlessly around the house for weeks afterward or sit quietly in their room as if in a daze. Some children do not believe the news, denying that the separation will happen because they are afraid to think about the end of their familiar world.

Expecting their children's strongly negative reaction to news of divorce, parents delay telling young people about it. They feel enough hurt already and do not want to face more pain and anger from their children. Divorcing parents feel worn down and without the emotional energy to deal with unhappy children, too. Adults tell themselves that marital problems should remain hidden from children to protect them from feeling insecure. In addition, parents want to keep intimate matters private, and they are right to do so; sexual matters or private disappointments deserve to remain between the couple alone. While keeping certain issues private, however, parents sometimes put up a false front about all areas of conflict, denying to their children that major problems exist at all. They tell themselves that the children are too young to know the details of divorce as an excuse to avoid embarrassment and guilt and to keep from becoming targets of the children's anger.

Although parents try to cover up the divorce plans, they rarely deceive the children. The pretense simply adds to the stress and damages the children's trust in their parents. The immediate pain at hearing about the divorce is less upsetting in the long run than the worry and distrust built by parental secrecy.

When they are told, children often respond so strongly to news of divorce in part because parents do not tell them enough. Wanting to have the crisis over as soon as possible, not wanting to burden children with private details, and wanting to protect the children's image of them, many divorcing parents say little beyond "We're getting a divorce and one parent is moving out."

Children need to know from both parents that the divorce represents a planned and thoughtful solution to years of obvious or hidden unhappiness. They need to know that the decision has been difficult and long thought out. They need to hear their parents' logical reasoning stated as honestly and directly as possible. Children need to hear that they will be able to keep meaningful relationships with both parents. They need reassurance that while husbands and wives divorce each other, parents do not divorce their children. They need to know where they will live. They need to know as much as possible except for intimate marital issues. What is more, parents should state the truth as calmly and matter-of-factly as possible, without "bad-mouthing" of either parent.

In addition, parents should give children the chance to voice their fears and concerns about the matter and should answer questions as honestly as they can. The young people will need to hear all this again and again over the following days, weeks, and years as they try in their own way and at their own level to understand and finally accept the divorce.

The less information children have about their parents' divorce, the more confused and upset they are. They fantasize about which parent is to blame for the tragedy. They imagine the worst possible reasons, which cannot be confirmed or refuted. They imagine that Dad is leaving because Mother prepared dinner too late or did not pick up his laundry on time. Children imagine Mom is leaving because Dad left the lawnmower outside during a thunderstorm. Children even imagine that they caused the divorce by misbehaving. They feel guilty, ashamed, and worthless. Children without enough information worry about how Dad will prepare his meals or whether Mom's salary will be enough to pay the bills. Adolescents worry about college plans, fearing that their future has been wiped out along with their family.

Furthermore, without enough information about the divorce, children do not understand or trust relationships. They become afraid of relationships and avoid becoming close to anyone else. How can one trust others if one day people love each other and suddenly, for no reason, they do not? Without confidence in themselves or in relationships, these young people will have hard times adjusting to a stepfamily.

There are no easy ways to tell children that their parents want to divorce. Putting on happy masks and forcing good cheer, with easy words about life being better, is no less than a lie, and the children know it. Life may get better for the adults, but right now it is not better for the children. Adults choose the divorce; children do not. Everyone feels miserable. Divorce is a sad event, and no glossing it over helps to change that.

If parents express sincere belief that this solution is well thought out and its goal is to bring relief and eventual happiness for one or both parents, they can better help their children adjust. If parents remain willing to answer all children's concerns in honest, caring ways, at least the children can keep trusting their parents. They can continue to see their parents as individuals who will answer their questions and keep them safe even if they do it from two different households. Children need to trust their parents if they are to feel confident about dealing with the larger world. Divorce need not disturb this vital link between adults and children. People can adapt to change if their basic sense of trust and security remains whole. What is more, if children cannot trust their parents to tell them the truth, to answer their questions, to be patient and understanding about their confusion and hurt, and to be available in times of pain, they cannot allow themselves to trust a stepparent later.

Jeff is one young man upset because his parents told him too little about their divorce. He pulled the top off a can of cola but could not take the first swallow. Jeff sat on the kitchen stool, trying to figure out what had happened. Last week Dad had told him about the divorce and that he had already moved into his own place. That was all. Where was Dad living? He did not even give Jeff his address or phone number. How could Jeff reach him? What was the problem with Mom, anyhow? Jeff's parents argued at times, and Dad took long business trips, but so what? Did Mom do something wrong? Was Dad the one? Or was it Jeff's fault?

Jeff was a strong-willed young man of fourteen and never was afraid to ask for what he wanted. But now he was afraid to ask Dad for more information. He did not want to upset him or make him angry. Mom did not seem to want to talk about the divorce, either. She acted as she always did, never saying a word about Dad or their problems. The more Jeff thought, the less he knew. He kept going around in circles, feeling worse with every turn.

## *How Children Feel After Divorce*

Children feel many emotions after their parents separate. Sometimes the feelings last for weeks or months, sometimes even longer. The feelings are bad enough, but not understanding that they are natural and normal responses to a sad situation makes children feel worse about themselves. Not understanding their emotions also makes it difficult for parents and stepparents to live with the children and have the patience to help them feel better.

Separation from one parent frightens children. They feel helpless and vulnerable. The world seems less predictable and reliable, and they worry about who will take care of them. They worry about how the single parent will manage to keep them fed, clothed, sheltered, and loved. They worry about their parents' health and emotional well-being. They worry about moving, changing schools, balancing household budgets, and about their parents' possibly remarrying.

Children also worry whether their relationship with the absent parent will end, fearing that each visit might be the last. The more chancy and less frequent the visits, the greater this fear. Children worry that one parent's anger will force the other parent to stay away forever. Others worry that the parent with whom they live will also leave them. They are terrified whenever the at-home parent walks out of their sight, goes shopping, or attends parties. A few children cannot sleep, afraid the parent will slip out during the night.

These children feel tremendous sadness. Their enormous loss brings frequent tears. They feel moody, unhappy, and restless. Some no longer want to play. Some feel ill and complain of stomachaches or headaches. A few children feel so empty that they want only to eat and eat to fill up the lonely space inside them.

For some young people, all thoughts turn to getting their parents back together. The less children know about the reasons for divorce, the more they dream about reuniting their parents. The very act of thinking about reuniting them lessens the pain of loss by linking the parents mentally, at least. The yearning to put the family back together or bring the absent parent home does not depend on the child's having a wonderful relationship with the absent parent. Often children want even abusive and critical parents to return because they want their life to feel intact again. Remarriage puts an unwanted end to this dream of regaining their first family.

Children of divorce feel twice rejected. One parent now lives out of the house and seems less interested in the children. No matter what the adults say, children feel abandoned. Meanwhile, the at-home parent is deeply involved in working full time, keeping meals on the table, and trying to build a new social life and shows little interest in the children right now. Never before have the children felt so lonely, and they question their lovability and worth. They deeply miss both parents and wonder whether their bad habits or bad character are the cause of their parents' lack of interest.

Usually, the parents' lack of interest reflects only the new arrangements of two households and two busy schedules. Living as a single parent is physically and emotionally demanding, particularly in the beginning with a new routine, a new job, and new activities to organize. Although children feel lonely and left out, the parents do not intend to push their children aside. There is a difference between being away and abandoning.

Unfortunately, a few parents do physically or emotionally leave their children. Some try to keep contact with their children, but the ex-spouse discourages or forbids it. Some try to keep contact but their angry, confused children make visits unpleasant. Some parents are so depressed about the divorce, their loss and failure, that even seeing the children reminds them of their shame. Other depressed parents seek to protect the children from knowing their hurt and sadness by staying away.

On the other hand, some parents tell themselves that they don't need their children. They want to spend their love, time, and money on their new family and put the past behind them. Thinking only of their own convenience, they want to live without responsibilities or memories of past mistakes. Parents who promise to visit often, who make dates to spend time together and then call them off or don't show up are the most selfish and hurtful of all. They say what is easy, what their children want to hear. They raise their youngsters' hopes and then are not there to see the disappointment, anger, and tears when the planned hour comes and the absent parent is nowhere to be seen.

Occasionally, relationships between the absent parent and the children waste away. The less often they see each other, the less sharing of activities, plans, and ideas occurs, the less the individuals know each other and the less they feel drawn to visit. Eventually, they become merely related strangers, and the blood ties become too little reason to continue seeing each other.

In other cases, a stay-away parent avoids seeing the ex-spouse because he or she is still angry about the divorce or jealous about the ex-spouse's new friends. The absent parent thus also gives up ties to the children who live with the other parent.

Whether staying away is deliberate or unplanned, children who feel rejected tend to think a lot about the parent who seems not to want them. They worry about what they may have done to push the parent away. Young people do not forget a natural parent because that parent no longer visits. Constantly thinking about the absent parent ties children to him or her in destructive ways. It leaves them with little interest or energy left over for seeking more satisfying relationships with friends and an interested stepparent.

Children whose parents divorce have other uncomfortable emotions. They feel torn between two parents they love. The parents, no matter how polite, still have deep divisions between them or else they would not divorce. Each parent stands for a side, and children feel pressure from themselves and from battling parents to decide which parent is right. Children love both parents but believe they cannot remain loyal to both. If they support one parent, they automatically betray the other. They do not want parents to be angry with them or love them less. No matter whose side the children take, they lose.

If children decide to remain neutral and take no sides, they risk both parents' anger. All alone in the middle, they have nowhere to turn for their own comfort and support. In the short run, choosing one parent to defend seems easier; at least that parent shows love and appreciation. As a result, many young people do side with one parent against the other, and they feel guilty, ashamed, and ripped in half.

Many children of divorcing parents also feel guilty about their own role in the separation. They wonder how much they added to the family's tensions. Children ages from six to twelve are more likely to feel that they caused the divorce. Older children often feel responsible only if they had a low opinion of themselves and strong doubts about their own value even before the divorce.

Not all children who feel guilty know that that is what they feel. Instead, some act angry or resentful, constantly arguing with adults in their world and giving friends a hard time. Young children have temper tantrums or hit other people. Older children speak sarcastically and in cutting ways. Some guilty-feeling children act cranky or rebellious, refusing to cooperate with household chores or accept family limits on behavior. They are so angry with themselves that they direct the anger outward toward others in unpleasant ways. At a time when they most need caring and understanding adults to help them forgive themselves for real or imagined mistakes, they push people away with their ugly attitudes and actions.

Anger after divorce stems not only from guilt about their own badness. Children of divorce frequently feel intensely angry at their parents. They feel angry at them for not having all the right answers, for failing at marriage. They feel angry at parents who tell them what is right and wrong, what is moral or immoral, but cannot act in right and moral ways in their own lives. Children feel angry with one parent for forcing the other to leave home, for giving them extra chores at home, for inconveniencing them, for making them do with less, for making them move into a new house or change schools or leave best friends behind. Young people feel angry with parents for showing little interest in them, for making them worry about budgets, bills, their health, or whether the car will be fixed in time for the next visit with their absent parent. Children feel angry because parents would rather spend time with other adults than with them. Finally, children feel angry with parents for forcing them to take sides, to feel lonely and scared, and for not getting back together as a family.

Children feel angry at their parents for betraying their trust in relationships, for taking away the safe predictability of the world, for making them doubt themselves and their relationships, and for making them feel so angry.

The tremendous anger that children feel does not automatically disappear when parents remarry. On the contrary, stepparents often become convenient targets for all the guilt, bitterness, and hurts these children have yet to express. A later chapter discusses this further.

*How Children's Age Affects Their Experience of Divorce*

While children who experience divorce share many common emotions, individuals react to divorce in their own ways. Their age also influences how divorce affects them. Younger children respond differently than do their older brothers and sisters. Children of three to five show fear, sadness, and confusion. They cannot fully understand the events taking place, although they know their parents are sad or angry. They see that one parent has moved out of the house. Young children feel almost totally dependent upon adult care and feel helpless without their parents' physical and emotional attention. Their fear leads them to cling to the remaining parent, crying wildly whenever he or she leaves for work, runs to the grocery store, or goes out on a date. Young children are reluctant to let the parent out of their sight for fear he or she will not return. They sometimes have a tantrum when the parent returns home, finally feeling safe enough to express their terror. Fear also makes bedtime into a problem because children worry that the remaining parent will be gone in the morning. Some children no longer want to go to their play group, terrified that no one will come for them when it is time to go home.

Feeling helpless and afraid, young children sometimes start acting like babies, playing with toys they outgrew months before, or soiling their clothes although they have been toilet-trained for a long time. They seem confused about real events, and they make up imaginary stories to explain their situation. This is especially true when overprotective parents have not told them enough reasons for the divorce. Young children wonder about their own specialness to their parents and ask if the absent parent will find a new family to replace the old one. Some young children pretend nothing bad has happened and insist that the absent parent is coming back. Others say they really do not miss the absent parent, pretending they do not feel loss. These children sometimes become angry and impatient, with temper explosions at home or at school. They begin hitting and fighting with friends or play games involving war and destruction. Others pretend they do not feel angry, and instead worry openly about something or someone hurting them.

In addition, young children often blame themselves for the family's separation, saying that they played too noisily or used bad manners at the dinner table. They crave the reassurance that comes from physical contact, and they climb into adults' laps, asking for hugs and kisses. These youngsters need adult protection and care and often respond quickly and well to a stepparent's comforting interest.

Children of six to eight understand the divorce more fully than do their younger brothers and sisters, although they do not totally grasp the details of what caused their parents to separate. They show more independence and mastery, and they are becoming successful in navigating their worlds at home and at school. They need their parents, but they are more self-sufficient than their younger siblings. These six- to eight-year-olds feel the grief and sadness of loss. They cry often but usually in private, not wanting to embarrass themselves in front of friends or teachers. While they may not fantasize about someday magically reuniting their original family, they occasionally worry about being sent away to live with strangers or waking up one morning and finding themselves without any sort of family. These young people feel deprived because something important to them is being taken away. Nevertheless, they focus on food, toys, clothing, and other items in their world as objects to obtain and keep. They cannot control a parent's leaving, but they can control how much food they eat or how many toys they have safely stored in their bureau.

Brothers and sisters of this age truly miss their absent parent, and nothing feels right since Mom or Dad left. Even if these children were not particularly close to the absent parent before the separation, even if they fought and argued all the time, children still deeply miss him or her. They talk about this parent all the time, as if that could help them feel that he or she were actually with them. Some children start acting like the missing parent, using the same gestures or words, wearing a left-behind sweater or hat. Again, they try to feel the absent parent's presence in words, thoughts, and actions.

These six- to eight-year-olds also are angry at their parents for turning everyone's life upside down. Many are afraid, however, to say anything mean or angry about the absent parent. That parent has already gone, and children this age fear that even secretly admitting their anger to themselves might make him or her never come back or stop loving them altogether. These children feel safer showing their anger toward brothers, sisters, friends, the remaining parent, and the stepparent. Those persons have not left; they remain handy targets for anger. In addition, the children realize that those persons care for them and will still care for them after angry outbursts.

Boys of six to eight, in particular, show great anger toward their at-home mother. Boys feel they have much in common with their Dad and think their mother's criticism of him, spoken or unspoken, also criticizes them. They are angry with their mother for driving Dad away. These boys secretly fear that since they are also men, mother will stop loving them as well. Boys want to defend their absent father. They do this by acting like him and saying mean things to their mother or hitting her, just as Dad used to do. They start dressing like Dad or mimicking his habits or ways of speaking.

Constant battling between boys and their divorced mother stands for many types of real anger. Boys are angry at their absent father and at their mother for making him leave. They want to stand up for and defend their absent parent. Boys challenge their mother to see if she will stop loving them and get rid of them too.

Only a few children of six to eight feel responsible for the divorce, but most would prefer to get their parents back together, even after one or both has remarried. Becoming part of a stepfamily does not immediately settle matters as far as these children are concerned.

Furthermore, these children feel strong loyalty conflicts. Many parents exepct them to take sides, choosing one parent over the other. Parents want their children's emotional support. They want to justify the rightness of their decision to separate, or they want to hurt the other parent by taking away the important relationship with the children.

Even without pressure from parents, children still feel torn apart by the need to take sides and to have one parent, at least, be right. If one parent is not right, why the divorce?

Children from nine to twelve also have special responses to divorce. They experience rapid physical and intellectual growth. Involved with school, sports, and friends, they have satisfying lives apart from the family. These enjoyable activities help keep some from feeling as if their entire world were coming apart. Older children understand what is happening in the family better than their younger brothers and sisters. They see their parents' strengths and weaknesses and realize that the divorce is between their parents rather than between parents and children. Although they may have disagreed with their parents and have heard them quarreling about child-raising issues, older children know that they did not cause the problems that split their family. They do not feel guilty about the separation. In fact, many children from nine to twelve see the benefits of their parents' divorce and are glad the bitterness, tensions, put-downs, and perhaps physical violence have finally ended. Because children nine to twelve show more physical and emotional maturity than their younger brothers and sisters, parents often expect them to take on more responsibilities. They suddenly find themselves doing a lot of baby-sitting for working or dating parents. They let themselves into an empty house after school and entertain themselves for a few hours until the parent returns from work.

In addition, parents confide in these young people, telling them intimate details and personal frustrations about the absent parent, about new boyfriends or girlfriends, and about the family budget. These youngsters often learn more about their parents' sex lives than they want to know. Parents begin leaning on them, asking for advice about friends, jobs, finances, and clothing. At times, parents want these older children to make decisions for them.

What is more, parents often expect these older children to take sides in marital conflicts. Since children nine to twelve act like parents' friends, they feel external and internal pressure to take up for one parent against the other. Taking sides becomes more of a problem when one parent still fights or is angry with the other; it forces them to turn against a parent they love. If one parent is right, they tell themselves, the other must be wrong. The children angrily attack the "bad" parent with cruel words, refuse to visit, and coldly reject gifts. While they feel glad they can attack the parent, the children also feel guilty and ashamed at their own meanness toward their once (and probably still) valued parent.

Flattered and feeling very grown up, these children have mixed emotions about their situation. They are proud that their single parent views them as mature. They do not want to disappoint the parent by refusing to accept responsibilities, by refusing to listen to private concerns, or by refusing to take sides against the other parent. But they are also afraid. They act confident, but they wonder how they will handle unexpected situations. What if the electricity goes out? What if the dinner burns? What if younger sister falls and hurts herself? These youngsters feel both able and scared at the same time. They feel proud, lonely, and trapped. Glad to be needed and respected, they are pleased with their new skills, but they also resent having no time or freedom for themselves or their own friends. When they actively take sides in battles between their parents, they feel terribly guilty.

Doug, age 11, had mixed feelings about his family. Doug was really acting like a grown-up. He, Dad, and his younger brother were making it okay even though Mom had left. Doug helped his brother get ready for school and became an expert at fixing scrambled eggs and french toast for breakfast. He was not so skilled preparing dinners, but no one was complaining. In addition, he and Dad were closer than ever. Dad asked Doug's advice about buying the new car, told him about problems at work, discussed the attractive women he dated, and revealed the real reasons why Mom had left.

Mom had always been warm and caring toward Doug, and he never imagined she had problems with Dad. She was a good liar, or she never could have started an affair with the man from the office. Doug no longer wanted to see her or talk with her on the phone. Yesterday, he had hung up when she called. Doug knew he had been mean, but he believed Mom deserved to be hurt the way she had hurt Dad.

Doug only wished he were older so he could be of more help to Dad. Dad counted on him, and he did not want to let his father down. Doug worried a lot about his family and his responsibilities, but he shrugged the worries off. "I guess that's what it means to grow up," he told himself.

While children nine to twelve can understand the family situation, many still are very angry at their parents' actions. Instead of feeling sad and helpless, older children strike out verbally or physically at their parents and teachers. They scold and criticize their parents' behavior. Aware of fairness and what is right and wrong, older children see their parents as acting unfairly and wrongly and forcefully tell them so. It is wrong to stop loving your husband or wife, and it is wrong to spend more time with dates than with your own children. It is not right to buy gifts for children in order to feel less guilty about the divorce. It is wrong to say mean things about the absent parent. It is not fair to stop making child-support payments simply to punish the former husband or wife. It is not fair that parents should be free to go out with friends but children must stay home and finish homework.

Sometimes, these children are angry with everyone and everything. They yell, scream, and constantly complain. They leave their room in a mess. They refuse to obey normal household rules and challenge all attempts to discipline them. A few harass their classmates by stealing pencils, pushing, punching, and being rude. Their anger occasionally takes the form of headaches, stomachaches, or leg cramps. Others feel restless and constantly engage in vigorous activity.

For many of these children anger covers deep sadness and helplessness. Because they like to feel in charge of their lives, they find it easier to feel in control with anger and keep-busy activities than to feel weak with their real despair. They like to think of their world in terms of "my" family, "my" friends, "my" school because these things tell them who they are. Divorce confuses these issues, and nothing seems clear. Divorce shakes their sense of who they are, because nothing is as it was. As the foundation of their world falls apart, anger helps these children hold themselves together. Anger helps them save face and feel as if they can still influence their lives, even if they do it in hurtful ways. Furthermore, this anger does not instantly disappear when one or both parents remarry. Angry children simply gain more reasons to be angry.

Finally, adolescents, ages thirteen to eighteen, have their own ways of responding to divorce. They have different relationships with parents than do younger children. Adolescents have independence and many skills to help them succeed outside the family. They no longer idealize their parents as all-powerful or view them as totally ignorant. They see their parents as unhappy persons, able to be hurt. They view parents as separate persons to be admired or despised for their very human behavior. They more fully understand the problems that led to the divorce. They have realistic ideas about money and can adapt to new budgets in their single-parent family. Teens also can be sympathetic and supportive to their unhappy parents without dwelling on their problems.

For adolescents, divorce often speeds up independence and maturity. The family crisis sometimes forces greater maturity as teens accept responsibilities for child care, cooking, and cleaning. Teens learn to make decisions because they realize no one is going to do it for them. Teens learn to be good companions and make thoughtful suggestions. The crisis also brings maturity as teens think about their parents' mistakes and draw accurate conclusions about how they can do better in their own lives.

Frequently, these young adults have the advantage of emotional space from their families. Their independence, increasing self-sufficiency, and outside friends help adolescents keep at a distance from family tensions. More and more, teens plan activities away from home with school functions, friends, and part-time jobs. Having satisfying things to do away from home and being aware of themselves as persons with their own life to lead, helps young adults avoid being pulled into the middle of family crises. They let their parents handle their own problems.

Other teens quickly develop this emotional distance when their family separates. They put on a cool manner and step outside the family's tensions. Teens escape stress at home by taking on more responsibility for their own life elsewhere. In this way, many teens avoid the pain, put-downs, and drain at home.

Nevertheless, adolescents do not have all the skills and attitudes they need for total independence. They have periods of confidence and maturity and periods of confusion and indecision. Many still need a stable family where they can retreat, reflect, and recover, gain encouragement and advice, and then return to the larger world.

Divorce removes this safe and secure home base. One parent has gone, and the other seems too busy with his or her own life to listen to teenagers. Parents may be changing faster than their teens, wearing new clothes, sporting new hairdos, and testing new life-styles. When mother comes downstairs wearing her daughter's new outfit and asks to learn the latest dance steps, or when father starts growing sideburns and trades his Ford for a Porsche, they no longer seem like the old comfortable parents teens knew yesterday. Preoccupied with their own lives, parents now have less time for sharing the young people's concerns or solving their problems. A single parent often enforces less discipline and maintains fewer controls.

Many times teens feel that they are pushed into complete independence before they are ready. Given more chores to assist a busy parent, they lose their fun times with friends. Teens resent the parent's behavior and feel as if he or she is competing with them. A parent wearing the latest fashions, bringing home young, attractive dates, and trying to look "cool" or "cute" turns teens off.

In addition, teens experience many of the same feelings and problems as do their younger brothers and sisters. Many feel tremendous loss and emptiness, cry frequently, feel run down and tired, and have difficulty keeping their attention on schoolwork. Teens face loyalty conflicts when parents expect them to take sides. When teens do give total support to one parent, that supports tends to last only for a year, a shorter time than for younger children in the same situation. Some teens decide not to tear themselves apart by taking sides, however, and pull away from both parents rather than selecting one over the other.

Teens often are angry at their parents for acting childishly and resent their selfishness. Teens do not like for their parents to show more interest in their work and new friends than they do in their own children. Angry young people sometimes turn that anger against their parents' lovers, who seem to be receiving the affection and attention that the teens believe should be theirs alone. At times, adolescents are extremely angry at the parent who wanted the divorce, no matter how good the reasons. On the other hand, teens sometimes are very angry at the parent who least deserves the anger and defend the parent who had acted badly during the marriage.

As with their younger brothers and sisters, sometimes the anger is justified. Parents do act in selfish and insensitive ways. At other times, the anger seems like the best solution because the real emotions of emptiness and powerlessness are too frightening for teenagers supposed to be "in control."

Frequently, adolescents have difficulty with sexual issues. With maturing bodies, they become aware of themselves as sexual people and have strong erotic feelings. They are learning how their bodies and thoughts respond as men and women, and they do not feel totally at ease about themselves in these ways. Adolescents worry whether they are attractive enough to the opposite sex and begin trying out new ways of acting. As if they did not have enough to think about concerning themselves as sexually maturing persons, they now see their parents as sexual people, too.

Most parents in a first family are used to their long-time sexual relationship with their spouse and feel less urgency about touching, hugging, and flirting. Sex plays an important but private role. Children of divorced parents, however, see their parents acting coy and seductive with dates. Young people share the bathroom with sleep-over lovers and occasionally hear stories about their absent parent's sexual behavior from their angry at-home parent. Teens know what is going on when they see a parent's date pull out of the driveway at 4 a.m. Moreover, teens meet their parent's lovers, who sometimes look young enough to attract their own sexual interest.

Seeing their parents openly behave as sexual people upsets many adolescents and makes the parent seem like a stranger. This is not the comfortable old Mom or Dad they knew before the divorce. It does not feel right for parents to act this way, and it embarrasses teens. Thinking about their parents as sexual people makes teens feel nervous, outraged, turned off, angry or excited themselves. It makes some envious, wanting the attractiveness, assurance, and experience their parents have. Teens often feel encouraged or challenged to become sexually active as well.

Many teens worry about sex and marriage in their own future. They worry about their sexual attractiveness and their ability to please a partner. They worry whether they will ever be able to feel comfortable about sex since they feel so turned off right now. Teens wonder whether they will ever marry, or they talk about delaying marriage at least until they are thirty. If they do marry, they say, they will not want children, who might be hurt by a divorce just as they have been. Not wanting children also allows young people to postpone the idea of having sexual relationships.

For adolescents, divorce promotes maturity and independence or brings it to a stop. Given more responsibility at home, they gain important skills and confidence, especially if they can keep an emotional distance from their parents' battles. Teens seek outside activities that take them emotionally and physically away from homebound stress. When their parent remarries, these teens fight against the closeness that a stepparent seeks to make the new family feel like a whole family. These adolescents earned their independence the hard way and do not want to give it up for a stepparent.

For other teens, increased jobs at home including giving emotional support and comfort to a confused and suddenly helpless parent means letting go of their own friends, interests, and outside activities. As the parent depends more and more on them, the young people spend more time and energy protecting the adult. They stop building separate identities and the skills needed for their own separate lives. In a few years, these teens may explode into defiant rebellion in attempts to break loose.

Finally, since upset parents find it difficult to set and enforce limits, teens sometimes find themselves with many strong impulses but without guidance or boundaries. The strict disciplinarian is gone—either out of the house or now more concerned with his or her own life than with acting as a parent—but teens still lack the ability to think things through before acting. If these young people also are angry with their parents for letting them down, they can find many hurtful ways to get revenge. Teens also resent a stepparent's taking over their jobs at home, receiving most of the parent's interest and affection, and setting new family rules and limits.

*Conclusion*

Parents divorce for many reasons. Some divorces are expected and even welcomed. Some divorces come as a terrible shock to children, relatives, and friends. But all divorces have real factors that led to the adult decision to break up the family.

Children need to know what problems led to their parents' decision to divorce. They do not need to know every intimate detail of their parents' lives, but they do need to know that their parents see divorce as a solution to a difficult situation. Children also need enough information to keep them from fantasizing that they were to blame or that they somehow failed to keep their parents' marriage together. Parents must explain the what's and why's as much as possible so children can understand that the divorce is between the adults, not between the adults and the children.

The more parents can explain the issues in the divorce, the more they can reassure their children of their love. Children need to be sure that both parents will still love them and spend time with them and keep them safe. Although words need to be followed by actions, parents can help their children feel more secure if they provide some real details as soon as possible. Children also need to be able to trust their parents, now more than ever. Children who are able to trust their parents' ongoing care and support are more willing to trust in a stepparent's care and support, too.

# CHAPTER III

*Living In a Single-Parent Family*

The Census Bureau reported in 1988 that nearly one out of every four American children under age eighteen, or 24 percent, lived with just one parent. This affected 14.8 million young people. It was 2.5 times more youngsters living with one parent than in 1960. Of these single-parent families, 89 percent of the children lived with the mother and 11 percent lived with the father. Sixty-six percent were formed after a divorce or separation; 7 percent were formed after the death of a parent.

Death or divorce brings important changes to family life. Economic changes result from loss of one parent's income. One paycheck no longer routinely comes to cover expenses. Even child-support and alimony payments do not stretch as far or arrive as often as the single-parent family needs. Divorce can reduce a single mother's income by 70 percent. Most husbands and wives have less money available. When divorce has led to a division of community property, a single-parent family finds itself without the same house, without the extra car. Less money means changing schools, leaving friends, and doing without. It means both parents working full time away from home. It means plenty of worry about budgets and the future.

Single-parent living usually means important changes for mothers. Many begin working full time. Some mothers enjoy the opportunity to make a career that was put aside while they remained at home with the children. Other mothers, particularly older women, bitterly resent having to work when they are not professionally or emotionally prepared.

With a mother's increased responsibilities outside the family, members find ways to do the jobs she did before she started working. Frequently, older children pitch in with cooking and cleaning chores while the parent finds a baby-sitter for the preschoolers. Mother or father drops them off at the sitter's on the way to work and picks them up afterward. School-age children either go to a neighbor's house after 3 p.m. or play at home for the two hours until the parent returns.

In addition, a single parent now makes all the important decisions alone. The parent decides whether to stay in the home or move, whether to buy a new washer and dryer or keep repairing the old ones. The single parent must decide whether to seek employment full time or part time or return to school in the hope of obtaining a better-paying, more satisfying job later. The single parent must decide what rules and limits should be set and enforced for the children and follow through with fair, consistent discipline. He or she must keep answering the children's questions about the breakup and reassuring them of their parents' continued love. A single parent makes all these and more important decisions at the very time when he or she is emotionally drained from the death or divorce and has few energy reserves left.

Children watch their single parent going through emotional changes. Some changes are positive. The parent feels elated and relieved to have finally solved the marriage problems through divorce, with no more battling, bitterness, or arguments. The parent senses a new beginning for both the adult and the children. Free from the trap of a bad marriage, the parent eagerly begins living his or her own life again, accepting the initial confusion and uncertainty at home as necessary steps on the way to a stable, secure, and satisfying future.

Another single parent experiences sad emotional changes. Depressed, lonely, and angry, still involved with the ex-spouse about the legal details of the divorce, this single parent argues about who gets what, hears himself or herself accused of poor parenting, and sees himself or herself as a failure at marriage. The single parent constantly criticizes the other parent for breaking their agreement, for not sending the alimony and child-support checks on time, for not caring about the children, and for finding another person to love.

Even after the divorce is final, depression sometimes continues. Single parents feel incompetent, unattractive, and worthless. Some spend whole days in bed or develop physical or mental illnesses. Tired all the time, they have no energy for parenting. No longer do family members eat meals together. Children go to bed or take baths whenever they want. They frequently are late for school, and their homework is undone. The house looks messy and totally disorganized. Unhappy, depressed parents rarely talk with their children and do more shouting and less listening when they do communicate.

Most single parents, however, do not become so depressed, although they often feel sad and find it difficult to stay on top of events at home. Until parents regain their balance, children step in to help with household duties. Young people act as advisers, friends, and helpers to their single parent. They want to do their part and do what they can to support the parent and keep the family going. They learn useful skills and build maturity in efforts to assist at home.

Unfortunately, when a single parent remains unable to function as a parent, children believe that both the home and the parent become their responsibility. They worry about leaving the parent alone, and take care of the parent when he or she becomes sick. They truly want to help, and they take pride in their growing ability to do so. But children also wish to get rid of some of the burdens they accepted at such a young age.

Natalie was such a person who picked up where her single-parent mother left off. No one complained about Natalie's cooking anymore. Her younger sisters used to gripe and tease her about raw meatloaf or soggy spaghetti, but now they sat quietly at dinner and ate. Sometimes Mother joined them, but she spent most of the time in her bathrobe since Dad left. Ten-year-old Natalie, the eldest, put herself in charge.

Natalie was proud of how well she took over, preparing meals, bathing the little ones, and bringing aspirin and orange juice to Mom. Natalie only wished her teachers understood why studying for tests or completing her reports did not seem important anymore. Whenever she felt nervous about all her new chores, wondering whether she was performing well enough, Mother would tell her how proud she was of Natalie's maturity. That made Natalie feel terrific. Mom's words helped her get through the hard times, but she wished Mom would get better soon. Until then, nothing else mattered.

## Visiting Absent Parents

Another big change after divorce involves visiting arrangements between children and their absent parent. Instead of sitting down together to breakfast and dinner everyday, watching TV together, or casually passing each other in the hall, children now see one parent, usually their father, about once a week, twice a month, or for long vacations. Instead of daily contact where children and parent know each other's activities and moods, one parent now loses intimate, ongoing contacts with the children.

The type of relationship the parent and children shared before the divorce does not always affect the frequency of visits. A parent who had close and loving bonds with children visits them often and regularly—or appears only once in a while. A parent who showed little interest before the divorce now realizes how much he or she loves and needs the children and visits often, developing a close relationship because the parent and the children truly miss each other. The amount of visiting depends on the persons involved, what they want from the relationship, and the distance between their two households. A parent who moves across town has more chances to see children than if he or she moves across the country.

Visiting an absent parent takes planning, coordination, and goodwill by the children and both parents. It helps a great deal when mother, father, and children all want to keep meaningful relations between parents and children. It takes a lot of arranging and flexibility on everyone's part. A time that is convenient for one parent may interfere with plans the other parent or children have already made. Yet if all the persons involved really want to maintain the relationship, they gladly work out the details.

At first, children may feel uncomfortable in the absent parent's new home, which looks and feels different from the other home. When they bring familiar toys or friends and spend several hours there, they become more at ease. Children make the visits easier for themselves and their parent when they stop being angry with the parent for leaving the family. Loving the parent and feeling angry at the same time ties children into knots and makes visits stressful. Angry children fear that the parent will stop loving them, but the emotions do not easily go away when they remind themselves of the parent's unfairness. It also helps when parents stop being angry with each other and show confidence and trust in each other's ability to be a caring and responsible parent.

Parents need flexibility in planning visits with children of different ages and different interests. Four-year-olds cannot be expected always to enjoy the same activities as ten-year-olds. Visiting parents need to recognize their children's uniqueness and make adjustments. They should plan activities they know will please both age groups; plan special experiences for one child one week and the other child the next; and allow children to bring friends along for company during the visits or plan visits with each child separately. A combination or alternation of plans works well.

Missing the intimate sharing that comes with daily living, an absent parent often tries to turn each visit into a carnival, working hard to entertain and please the children. Movies, trips to the skating rink, gifts galore follow in an effort to give children memorable and enjoyable visits. An absent parent wants the children's love, affection, and loyalty. He or she tries to make up for lost time and buy pleasure at the expense of parenting. Rules no longer seem important, discipline grows lax, and children do as they please. The parent does not want to spoil the special mood of the visits by setting and enforcing limits.

Children learn to behave one way at home and differently with their visiting parent. Children and parents, however, learn that true, satisfying relationships grow from quiet times when they discuss their ideas, retell events in their lives, and share their dreams and fears. Discussing what is important to each one comes more easily when doing ordinary things such as washing dishes, cleaning the attic, or simply sitting together on the front porch watching cars pass. After visits begin, many children and their absent parent settle into ordinary, unexciting but deeply meaningful ways of being together.

Parents and children make problems for visiting in different ways. An angry parent greatly complicates the situation. When one parent still feels bitterness toward the other, the angry parent fouls up the visiting arrangements in attempts to hurt or punish the other. An angry parent sends children on errands before the visiting parent arrives. The visiting parent decides to leave without the children rather than wait for them in the same house with the ex-spouse. An angry parent forgets dates and times for visits so that children are not ready to go when the visiting parent arrives. An angry parent makes noisy, embarrassing scenes when the visiting parent arrives, criticizing his or her lateness, earliness, or late child-support checks. An angry parent scolds the ex-spouse about having sent children home last time wearing dirty clothes, complains about the ex-spouse allowing them to act wild, or yells about how cranky and unmanageable the children behaved when they returned from their last outing. The angry parent phones the visiting parent a few hours before the arrival time and says, untruthfully, that the kids are sick in bed or have homework to do and cannot go out that day.

In one study, half the at-home parents valued their children's visits with the absent parent and encouraged the relationship. Twenty percent did not think the relationship with the absent parent was good for the children and actively discouraged continued contact. Thirty percent had mixed feelings about the relationship, thinking it good in some ways, bad in others. They did not prevent their children from visiting with their absent parent but did not put themselves out to help arrange it, either.

At times, the absent parent also makes visiting troublesome. An absent parent may feel too depressed to see the children. Visiting the old home is too painful to endure. It brings back bittersweet memories. Although the absent parent may be a most loving parent, the sadness makes him or her feel too ill or tired to visit children regularly. The adult believes that this behavior protects the children from seeing his or her pain even while protecting him or herself from feeling it.

Another absent parent experiences much guilt about causing the family's breakup and upsetting the children. Many had close and caring bonds with their youngsters that were the only satisfying relationships they had in the family. The adult feels bad about having left and shame at the idea of facing the children at all. He or she let the children down and knows it. Many a guilty absent parent either stops visiting the children to avoid the embarrassment and guilt of facing them, or visits often in the beginning but rarely keep it up. A guilty parent is also likely to play Santa during visits, trying to buy the children's love and approval, to charm away their anger and hurt.

In truth, many an absent parent stops visiting the children out of shame over the pain he or she has caused them. Seeing the children, the adult feels a failure, and that makes him or her uneasy. No one likes to admit failure. People do not want constant reminders of their worst moments and their worst mistakes. Through no fault of their own, children remain living proof of their parents' failure to make marriage work. Some adults generally like themselves, forgive themselves for making even big mistakes, and learn to be better people from difficult experiences, but other adults cannot. They do not accept their own limits and errors nor take comfort from those areas in life in which they succeed. Instead, they feel the need to reject the mistakes and everyone attached to them. They pretend to themselves that they never failed, never hurt anyone. To keep up this pretense and false image of themselves, the adults refuse to continue seeing their children: If they pretend they have no children, they also pretend they never failed.

In these cases, children are not to blame if the absent parent is too weak and immature to accept the truth and make the best of it. Nevertheless, when an absent parent stops visiting or visits only now and then, children hurt even worse than if they could spend time with this parent and work out satisfying bonds on new terms beyond anger, blame, and guilt.

Elaine's father could not accept his failure at marriage, but Elaine did not realize his problem. She was ashamed to show her mother the report card: four D's and two F's—an impossible set of grades for a tenth grader usually on the Honor Roll. Since Elaine's Dad had moved out, she thought about him all the time. At home, in class, washing the dishes, watching TV, he was always on her mind.

They had had such fun together in the old days, but now she did not even know where he lived. Mother acted as if Dad had never existed. Dad had told Elaine the divorce would not mean he loved her less, and he promised he would see her often, but he lied. Elaine worried about him, wondering if he were okay, and asked herself if she had done something wrong to make him stop caring.

During the weekend, Elaine visited her grandmother, Dad's mother. Her grandmother tried to comfort Elaine by telling her what a winner her Dad was. The divorce had badly shaken his confidence because he had never failed at anything before. Returning to his old home and seeing Elaine made him feel very bad because he remembered the mess he had made of his marriage. This information did not make Elaine feel any better. She just kept wondering, over and over, where he was and what she had done wrong.

In addition, the visits with an absent parent sometimes upset the children. Seeing their parents argue with each other again bothers them. Older children are especially likely to see their angry parents fight, because parents often protect younger brothers and sisters from such ugly outbursts.

Other children have mixed feelings about the visits. They dearly love and miss the absent parent but still are angry at him or her for leaving. They are disappointed by their absent parent's lack of interest in seeing them more often and are angry and sad at the same time.

In other situations, children feel close to their at-home parent. If they know or suspect that the parent resents the absent parent, they are afraid to visit or enjoy him or her. They do not want to upset the parent with whom they live.

Still other children remember how sad they feel when time comes to say goodbye and they must return to their regular home. To avoid feeling unhappy later, they decide not to visit in the first place. These children feel upset if they go and upset if they stay; they cannot win.

When a parent occasionally pushes children away, children sometimes do the same to the parent. Having a parent stop loving them feels worse than any tragedy that could possibly happen. Young people hurt like crazy but cover up their pain with anger. They do not like feeling shut out or dropped, so they do the dropping first. They save face by saying, "Who needs Mom or Dad, anyway!" They tell themselves the parent does not matter, and they try to believe it: If the parent does not matter, they will not hurt so much if the parent stops loving them. They feel angry at the parent because feeling angry makes them feel in control. It makes them feel that they are the ones who choose to let the other go rather than the ones whom the parent reject.

Teens who feel their absent parent's rejection tell themselves that two can play that game. They feel bad about themselves because they believe they were not worthy of continued love and interest.

Teens sometimes cannot see their parent's weaknesses and limits, so they blame themselves for the relationship's going sour. These teens tell themselves that they do not like or need the absent parent anymore and make a great show of their independence and lack of concern. This pretense helps them feel better about themselves because now they are the ones in charge, they are the ones to drop the parent.

On the other hand, teens sometimes deliberately decide to reject their uninterested absent parent. They realize that he or she was never really interested in them, and that they never really enjoyed their visits. At this point in their lives, teens can stand apart and view the parent realistically as a separate person who is unreliable, selfish, unloving, and untrustworthy. These teens decide that they do not want to be like this parent, they do not want to be with this parent. They deliberately reject both the parent and the parent's values. When this happens, teens no longer become upset about the parent's lack of interest or affection. They wish the parent were different, a person more capable of loving and caring; but they know that is a wish and not the way things really are. They stop feeling angry and hurt and instead feel free to enter relationships with friends, other adults, and a stepparent able to give them affection, support, and a truly satisfying relationship.

Jack was one teen able to let go of his relationship with his uncaring absent parent. Jack, age fifteen, rolled over in bed and thought about the talk he had just had with his ten-year-old brother Tim about their Mom. Their parents had divorced five years earlier, and they had lived with Dad since then, visiting Mom on vacations. Two years ago she had accepted a job in another state, and they could not visit her often. Yet even before she had left, Mom did not visit very often, and making small talk with her was difficult. No one knew what to say, and they all felt uneasy. They did not feel close anymore.

Tim had told Jack that since he was ten years old and grown-up now, he did not need Mom anymore. Dad was doing fine as their only parent; he always made time to listen to them and mess around. If Mom really loved them, Tim added, she would not have taken that job. Tim was glad to have Mom out of his life once and for all.

Jack listened to his brother but did not believe a word of what he said. Jack knew how unhappy he himself had been when Mom left, how he had wished she could live closer and care more about them. At that time, he also had said he did not care about her. Now he felt differently. Mom was just a person who did not feel comfortable with intense relationships. She had always had difficulty showing affection to Dad or to the boys. She was nicer with strangers who did not ask so much of her emotions. Seeing her in this way, Jack did not feel bitter the way he used to. Mom was what she was, and no one could change that.

Teens do not need a lot of time with an absent parent to keep their relationship strong. One day or a few hours a week is enough for many adolescents. If they have close and caring bonds with this parent built during years shared together, whether living or visiting together, a few hours' contact a week keeps them close.

## Dealing With Parents' Boyfriends and Girlfriends

After divorce, a parent's needs often become completely separate from the children's needs. A divorced parent is engaged in many new activities from working, to running the household, to disciplining children singlehandedly. A single parent feels tired and lonely. He or she has been through sad and difficult times and wants to put the problems into the past. Many want to rebuild their own life as a professional and social person apart from the family. A single parent wants to feel confident about his or her abilities again and to do things that make him or her feel capable and attractive. A single parent's calendar overflows as he or she spends more time away from home, experiencing the first freedom in years.

Meanwhile, as the parent looks for satisfactions outside the home, the children need greater security and reassurance inside the home. They have been through difficult times, too, and look to the parent for continued love and attention.

The period between marriages brings conflict between parenthood and personhood. A single parent wants to have it all and looks for ways to begin life outside as well as to reassure the children with attention, guidance, and discipline. The fact is that a single parent has less time for children, choosing instead to spend more energies on personal needs. A single parent believes he or she has sacrificed and suffered enough and now has earned the right to put self first. Meanwhile, children feel ignored and lost. It seems as if they are losing both parents, not only the one who moved out. Young people want their parents to be happy, but not at the children's expense.

A single parent's social and sexual life changes after divorce. He or she is lonely after the separation. Old friends stop calling. Friends of both husband and wife do not want to anger either by taking sides. Other friends decide to stand by one and drop the other. In addition, many friends do not like the reminder that divorce can happen in any family, maybe even in their own.

Many times, a single parent feels unattractive and unworthy as a person. Divorce represents a failure in this important area of living. Many a single parent does not like him or herself very much and seeks chances to rebuild self-confidence. With dating, each meeting tells the single parent that another adult still finds him or her attractive. Furthermore, a divorced parent often feels betrayed by the opposite sex, and dating helps in starting to trust others again.

Sometimes a divorced parent has been involved in romantic relationships before the divorce. Unhappy with the marriage, the parent looked for affection with persons outside the family. Perhaps these outside relationships added fuel to the decision to divorce, giving the parent the courage and emotional support to end a bad marriage. Discovery by the other parent meant the end of trust between the couple, making divorce the next step. In any case, a parent with an outside relationship frequently breaks up with that person when the stress of divorce is over, no longer needing the relationship to make up for the unhappy ties at home. He or she may even blame the outside person for causing the problems at home. For another single parent, divorce means that he or she may now openly see the outside person and build an active social life around this once-secret relationship.

Whether a single parent begins dating people known before the divorce, has dates arranged by mutual friends, or sees people from work, he or she dates. One study found that the average divorced man dates fifteen to twenty women during the three years following divorce and the average divorced woman dates to seven to ten men. Many of the relationships are casual affairs; children see the person once or twice and never again. Other relationships grow into serious romances, and children see these persons often.

Whereas a single parent enjoys the new romance and the positive things it says about his or her desirability, children feel left out and abandoned, no matter how happy they are that their parent is in a good mood.

Seeing a parent acting "in love" makes many young people sick. Companionship is one thing, but all that touching, flirting, and giggling makes a parent look disgusting and ridiculous. At best, children have mixed feelings about their single parent's dating.

Children in a first family rarely become upset about their parents' sexuality. Parents have been married a long time and the excitement of love has mellowed. As a result, in some families children see less touching, hugging, or seductiveness between their parents. In other families, physical affection between parents looks familiar and comfortable. Children watch the hand-holding and kissing all the time, and it is nothing new.

When children see their single parent acting this way with strangers, they do not like it at all. For one thing, they view the affection as a betrayal of their absent parent. For another, they do not like to think of their parent as a sexual person. The mushy stuff looks gross and wrong, and the young people are embarrassed about it.

Children nine to twelve are particularly uncomfortable about their single parent's sexuality. As growing young people they do not yet feel at ease with themselves as sexual persons. Watching their parent engage in physical intimacies makes them nervous. They do not fully understand sex, and they are not ready to understand, either. Because they know so little about sex as physical and emotional closeness, any innocent show of affection such as a long goodnight kiss or tight hug seems like the start of an orgy.

What is more, children nine to twelve like rules, structure, and values that they can use to guide their own lives. They want to look up to the parent and follow his or her example. Children's strict morality about right and wrong, which they learned from their parents, often clashes with the single parent's new relaxed ideas about sex. Yesterday the parent said to save sex for marriage; today the children share the breakfast table with a sleepover date. Yesterday the parent said the children's bodies were private and nobody should touch them; today young people find the parent making out with a stranger on the couch in the den. These behaviors disgust young people and make them question the values their parents taught them. They react by completely turning off to sex in any form, or they feel challenged to begin their own sexual activities to see what all the fuss is about.

A single parent occasionally makes these situations even more difficult for the children. A parent may ask children to spy on the other parent's sexual activities and report about what goes on in the other home. "Does your mother see other men?" "How late does she return from her dates?" "Does he spend the night?" "Is your father seeing anyone special?" "Does she leave any clothes or makeup at his house?" These questions put young people in an unpleasant spot.

A single parent may also boast about his or her own sexuality. The parent talks with children about which clothes make him or her look sexier or how exciting certain dates are. The parent flaunts his or her sexuality by having a parade of dates in and out of the house and by letting lovers spend the night. These single parents are trying to feel good about themselves by proving to everyone, themselves and their children included, how attractive and desirable they are. After the self-doubts and shattered confidence of divorce, this behavior makes single parents feel valuable and special once more. It does not make their children feel that way.

Caught up in their own lives, single parents mean no harm to children by these actions. It is their way of patting themselves on the back while having enjoyable relationships. The behavior does, however, sometimes hurt children. The young people feel less important since the parent shows less interest and spends less time with them. It also heightens their awareness of sex before they are able to fully understand the difference between physical closeness and emotional closeness, between physical pleasure and genuine intimacy. Many children find themselves forced to think about sexuality before they are ready.

Sometimes a single parent's sexuality presents challenges to young people of the same sex. If this is what a real man (or woman) is supposed to do, and since I am a man (or woman), maybe this is what I am supposed to do, too. If Mother can attract a man with this behavior, so can I. If Dad can get adoring looks from attractive women by flirting, touching them, and buying gifts, so can I. The unspoken challenge sets many adolescents on the way to early sexual activities.

Other times, young people feel jealous about their single parent's new lovers, wanting the parent's attention and affection for themselves. Girls flirt openly with their mother's dates, testing the behaviors they see Mother use and at the same time gaining needed interest and attention from the men. Boys flirt teasingly with their father's dates, who are often younger and prettier than good old Mom. Furthermore, young people occasionally find themselves attracted to their parent's dates and enjoy the coy exchanges in their own right.

Now and then, children resent the dates very much. They do not want to share their parent's time and energies with these strangers. They wonder where the relationships are leading and how it will affect them. At times, young people dislike the dates as persons because they have unusual or different ways of doing things. Angry young people try to break up the parent's romances by finding fault with the friends' clothing, looks, or behavior. They refuse to be friendly and answer all questions with a cold "yes" or "no." They are rude on the phone when the dates call, letting them overhear, "Hey, Mom, it's Mr. Wrong" and "Dad, the lady with the tight dresses." They try to break up relationships by arguing with the dates when they arrive to see the parent or by wearing their rattiest clothes when they open the door. Young people show their anger at their parent's boyfriends and girlfriends in hundreds of spoken and unspoken ways. Even the nicest friends become suspect as young people think the show of friendliness toward them is only an act. This is especially true when the adults come on too strong in the beginning, gushing with smiles, hugs, and gifts before they really know the young people.

Sometimes young people find themselves causing problems between their single parent and a lover.

Ann felt blind fury at her mother and ran into her room. Mother's new boyfriend disgusted Ann. He was only a few years older than she, wore greasy flannel shirts and old cords, and had no class at all. He ate with his fingers, left beer cans all over the living room floor, put his feet on the table, and ignored Ann. To see him and Mom holding hands or sitting close together on the sofa made Ann want to vomit.

Ann felt ashamed of her Mom. Ann was a good judge of people, mature for seventeen after years of looking after herself since Dad had left; and she told Mom this guy was a loser. Mom did not say much in his defense, but she kept seeing him.

This time Mother took his side in an argument. Ann knew she had started the fight. She had planned all week to watch a certain show on TV and had promised to give a report on it in English class. He came to visit and wanted to watch the basketball playoff. They had only one TV, and Ann begged her mother to let her see the special show. The boyfriend sat in the armchair, grinning as the playoff began. Ann walked over to change the channel, but he struck her arm away from the dial. Ann was stunned, and she cried for Mom to throw him out of the house. Mom told her to sit down and leave the TV as it was.

Ann could not believe her ears. Mom chose that slob over her own daugher! How could she, Ann sobbed as she sat alone in her room.

Single parents have difficulty being two people at once. Feeling romantic, attractive, and attentive as lovers conflicts with their need to be parents who can set and enforce rules for their children. Arguments between their dates and their children put parents right in the middle. Whichever side the parent chooses, someone loses. It is hard to seem kind, appealing, and tactful while yelling at rude children to clean up the den and start preparing for bed.

Young people see their parent's dilemma and deliberately create fusses to put the parent on the spot, hoping to upset his or her romances.

A parent responds by using outside help, hiring housekeepers so as to be free from home longer yet have the children under an adult's watchful eyes. A parent asks grandparents or relatives to watch the children for the weekend or considers sending them to boarding school or summer camp. When forced to choose, some single parents choose their lover over their children because the need to be part of a warm adult relationship is more important at the time than the need to be a parent.

No matter how children work to break up their parent's romances, few succeed. Few affairs end simply because children do not want them to last. When a parent has doubts about a new relationship, children's protests serve as extra encouragement to end it. On the other hand, when a parent really enjoys a new relationship and wishes to continue building it, he or she listens to children's gripes but goes ahead with the romance. Some parents believe that when young people get to know the new adult better, they will like him or her. Others believe themselves entitled to see whomever they want and will do so whether their children like it or not.

In any case, any new marriage will have to work for children, too, or it will not work. A single parent cannot marry as a childless person. Considerate and wise parents look at remarriage with an eye to their children's feelings and future adjustment. They weigh their children's opinions and emotions very heavily in the decision to remarry. If a single parent wants a new marriage to succeed, he or she must consider the children's feelings now and later. The fact that the divorce rate for remarriage is higher than that for first marriage supports this.

Children, however, should not have the final say in whether or not their single parent remarries. Young people should be told well in advance of remarriage so they can prepare themselves emotionally and become more at ease with the idea. A stepparent-to-be should reach out to the children gradually, begin to know them as persons, and start developing relationships with them. When young people actively seek to break off their parent's romances, they usually make life difficult for everyone involved, including themselves, because they miss the chance to have their parent happy and miss the chance to build ties with an interested adult who may someday become a friend and a respected, loved person.

*Why Parents Remarry*

Even when children see their single parent involved in a new relationship, even though they see their parent showing affection and serious interest in a new friend, learning about remarriage comes as a shock. Remarriage is a different situation altogether. While the parent feels elated about remarriage, many children hear the word as bad news.

Remarriage means many upsetting things to young people. If they are still disturbed about the death or divorce and wonder if they are unlovable because one parent left them, remarriage means the loss of the remaining parent. Living in a single-parent family brings parent and children together, helping each other with household chores, giving each other emotional support. Many children become very close to their single parent during months and years of living together. They share a special tie that helps them survive difficult times: "We against the world!" Remarriage means that the parent with whom the young people had become so close now shows interest and affection elsewhere. The parent seems to be choosing another adult in place of them. Young people fear that remarriage will break the last important bond with their remaining parent; they will be abandoned again, and nobody will love them. Children also ask themselves why, if their single parent really loves them, he or she would want to love someone else?

These young people do not realize that love comes in unlimited amounts and in many forms. People are always able to give more love. The more they give, the more they have to give. Love is not like apple pie in which pieces are served until no more remains. In addition, the love a parent feels for children is not the same love the parent feels for other adults. Parental love is not the same as husband-wife love, so the two relationships can never compete. In fact, the happier a person is as a husband or wife, the happier the person feels in the parental relationship.

Remarriage also means another type of loss for children. If their single parent marries again, he or she will no longer be free to remarry the first spouse, the children's other parent. Many children dream about getting their parents back together. They hope for it, wish for it, and pray for it. Even as years pass, children play with the idea of reuniting their "real" family. Thinking about it makes them feel good, as if they were actually back in their first family once more. When these young people hear that their single parent plans to marry a stranger, they lose this special dream and become very sad.

"Second marriages represent the triumph of hope over experience," commented Dr. Samuel Johnson several hundred years ago. He meant that although people know the practical problems involved, they go ahead in the hope that all will work out successfully. A single parent has failed once at a most important relationship but stands ready to risk marriage once more. Single parents risk remarriage in large numbers: Five out of six divorced men and three out of four divorced women remarry within three years.

This important step represents an emotional issue as well as a practical and legal one. As exciting as the courtship may be, remarrying can remind a parent of the hurt, loss, and failure of the first marriage. A parent wants to do better this time but often fears making the same or different mistakes. A parent remarries for many reasons, some clearer than others.

Many parents learn much about themselves after divorce. They see where they demanded too much or expected too little from their first marriage. They look closely at their own faults and work to change themselves into people more able to love honestly and realistically. They now feel able to compromise when necessary but to stand firm for what they sincerely believe. Single parents miss the companionship, comfort, and sharing between two mature and caring adults. They want someone with whom to share their ideas and plans. They move to remarriage with the independence and confidence born of personal pain and personal growth.

Some single parents wish to remarry to prove to themselves and to others that they are not a failure. This time, they think, they will do it right. They want to rebuild their confidence, feel good about themselves again, and regain society's approval by having a successful marriage. As single parents, they feel lonely and strange in a society where everyone else seems part of a couple. They need the emotional and financial support that come from living with another adult. They realize that credit ratings, mortgages, and charge accounts go more easily to married people. Many believe that children need two parents in the home, and they feel drained trying to raise children by themselves. Some parents do not want to embarrass their children or their own parents by living with a lover without the legal and social sanction of marriage.

In addition, many adults want to marry a parent. Some of these individuals have never been married and do not have their own children. When they meet their new spouse's children, they like the young people's personalities, ideas, or looks. They enjoy the idea of having a ready-made family. It makes them appear successful to themselves and others. Many adults look forward to loving their stepchildren as dearly as if they were their natural children.

Some of these persons, however, have unrealistic ideas about what children and parenthood are really about. They believe they will be replacement parents to the children, and they expect the children to love and obey them as they would natural parents. These stepparents soon learn how wrong their ideas are, but the notion of instant family and togetherness seems romantic enough to encourage them to marry a person with children.

Unfortunately, while society has clear customs about first weddings with white gowns, veils, rice, and orange blossoms, planning a second wedding brings confusion. No clear rules or traditions point the way. A white dress can no longer stand for a bride's purity and chastity, since this bride has been married before and has children to prove her sexual activity. At first weddings, brides asked girlfriends to be bridesmaids, but now brides' friends are older and have their own children. First weddings usually see lots of relatives who come to share the day's joy. Second weddings, while happy events, also remind people of a first marriage's failure. Not all relatives and friends approve of divorce and remarriage, and they are less eager to celebrate than they were the first time. Deciding whom to invite and what to wear becomes complicated.

With remarriage, the couple must decide what plan suits them best without tested guidelines to show them the "proper" ways. As a result, a single parent plans a simple second wedding with only closest friends and relatives present. The couple wants a special day, but the ceremony marked by mixed feelings does not seem like a "real" wedding. Nevertheless, the ceremony signals the start of a new family and deserves enthusiastic and supportive send-offs.

As much as possible, a single parent should involve children with the wedding plans and let them take part in the ceremony. Marriage is between the couple, of course, but it also marks the birth of a second family for children. The more young people feel part of the marriage, the more they feel valued and included, the more they will support the new family. They feel that they are not losing a parent but gaining a second family.

# CHAPTER IV

## Becoming a Stepfamily

Making marriage work takes work. The people involved must be honest and dependable, sensitive and tolerant. They must be able to talk and listen carefully, show understanding of each other, and serve as companions, friends, and confidants. The couple decide how to do all the practical things that keep the household organized and running smoothly. They must be ready to cooperate and compromise. They must satisfy each other's sexual needs, be faithful, and desire to please each other. Each must willingly give total effort to the task and not keep score.

As if these tasks were not hard enough, couples facing remarriage carry extra baggage. They carry feelings of loss and pain from having failed once. They do not totally trust their own ability to form and maintain relationships and solid family lives. They bring with them children who are skeptical at best about what the new marriage means for them. So many issues have yet to be clarified or resolved. Persons with fixed ideas about what a second family will be like or with little ability to live with uncertainty find stepfamily life very difficult. Unrealistic ideas about what a stepfamily should be and the practical problems of dealing with the differences between a first and second family can make life rough going for all concerned.

### Stepfamilies Are Not Like First Families

By themselves, stepfamilies are not better or worse than first families, but they do differ. The more these differences can be recognized, understood, and handled, the greater the chances for building satisfying experiences for all stepfamily members.

*Different Family Models.* In the first place, the forms of stepfamilies differ from the forms of first families. They offer different models of family life.

In first families, natural parents and their children live together in the same house. The adults' relationship began long before the children's birth. They built a solid relationship together, and they became parents to the same children at the same time. Parents and children have years in which to care for each other, see each other in good moods and bad, and learn to love each other. In first families, children belong to only one household. They know who they are and where they belong.

Furthermore, since everyone in the home is biologically and legally related, family members have clear lines of responsibility. Everybody knows and accepts who is supposed to do what, to whom, and with whom. The family feels like "we."

It is easy to see how stepfamilies bring a model of family life that undoes many of these "givens." In stepfamilies, one of the children's biological parents is elsewhere, either deceased or living in another household. With two natural parents living under different roofs or with one parent alive only in memories, children face questions of where they belong, to whom they should remain loyal and loving, and whose rules they should obey.

In stepfamilies, the relationship between the children and one of the adults is longer and more complex than that between the two adults. Some household members share years of intimacy and close emotional ties while other members begin as strangers.

In stepfamilies, many members come together after experiencing loss of their first family. Members bring the fears, self-doubts, and strong emotions that loss stirs. Stepfamily members have separate pasts, different experiences, values, and traditions. They have different ways of seeing the world and of solving problems.

Timing in stepfamilies also presents differences. In first families, husbands and wives have months or years to share by themselves before their children are born. They have the time and privacy to learn more about each other and build close and loving bonds. In stepfamilies, husbands and wives do not have this time to grow close and build strong ties. They do not live alone; they live with children from the first day of their marriage.

From a distance, stepfamilies look like any other family with parents and children. Close up, stepfamilies present a different picture altogether. It is not necessarily a better or worse picture—just different. To pretend otherwise is a mistake.

*Different Experiences and Outlooks.* Many adults enter a second marriage with different experiences and outlooks than they had in their first family. No longer young and innocent, the spouses in remarriage know themselves better now. They have matured during the years of hurts and disappointments, and they know they are not perfect. They also know that their spouse is not perfect either. A remarried couple know what they want and do not want out of their marriage. They learned these things the hard way in their first marriages. Hopefully, they show greater tolerance for their own and other's weaknesses, recognize what qualities are truly important in a relationship, and do not become upset about minor irritations that might have bothered them in the first marriages. Experienced at marriage, they develop more realistic ideas about how to make the new relationship successful. Even if one partner starts out with a bad attitude about marriage from a first sad experience and expects to solve difficulties by walking out like the last time if it comes to that, the other partner often has learned more useful ways of coping in marriage. The realistic mate can help the discouraged mate deal with problems in more constructive and satisfying ways. As a result, they experience less disappointment or failure because they no longer expect perfection. Instead, they expect kindness, thoughtfulness, consideration, support, and understanding. Each partner does what needs to be done and less often assumes that certain jobs are "men's work" or "women's work." They act more flexibly and supportively to keep the household running.

Remarrying adults often have greater economic security because at least one partner has moved ahead in his or her career and earns a larger salary. Even with child support and alimony due to their first families, many stepfamilies have more money to spend than single-parent families.

Also important, many couples in stepfamilies have developed a sense of humor born of personal awareness and pain, which helps them keep their perspective. They are more willing to take life and problems as they come, instead of making a big deal out of everything. They change what they can and let the rest be. They are more likely to laugh at frustrations than explode at minor problems.

Furthermore, a remarried couple are willing to try harder to make their marriage work. Aware of their past errors, they do not want to repeat them. They feel the eyes of the entire community watching and waiting. They cannot afford to fail at marriage again.

In addition, more advance planning goes into preparing for remarriage than for a first marriage, especially because it involves children. In stepfamilies, parenthood comes before spousehood. Parents in stepfamilies make conscious efforts to do better for their own sake as well as for their children. At the same time, stepparents feel as if the whole world watches every action to see if they will be the cruel stepparents of fairy tales. Their success at this marriage will be their victory, showing outsiders and themselves alike that they were not the ones to blame for the end of their first marriage. Success in this marriage will prove them right, capable of building important ties. Successful remarriage means the divorce was not *their* fault.

*Expecting the Impossible*

Frequently adults and children enter stepfamilies with many unrealistic ideas about what attitudes and behaviors to expect from themselves and others. These unrealistic ideas affect the way adults and stepchildren relate to each other. They also affect the goals the individuals have for their new family.

*Instant Love.* Stepparents often expect to love stepchildren instantly as if they were their natural children. The moment they become stepparents, they plan to love the children "as if they were my own." Natural parents and society as a whole encourage this mistaken idea.

Instant and mutual love between stepparents and stepchildren rarely if ever happens. Most stepparents hardly know their stepchildren, let alone feel deep affection for them. Real love takes time and shared experiences to grow. Real love is based on respect and trust, and the emotion ripens slowly.

When instant love does not occur, stepparents feel guilty and think they must be doing something wrong. They want to love and be loved by their stepchildren. When this does not happen, they worry. At this point, some stepparents deny that they do not love their stepchildren. Some try treating both natural children and stepchildren the same to prove that no child is a favorite regardless of blood ties.

Stepparents suspect that the whole world watches every look, sees every action, hears every critical tone of voice and judges them. They also do not want their new spouse to criticize them. These stepparents bend over backward to be kind in attempts to prove the love they do not feel. As a result, they do not feel comfortable showing any real "negative" emotions such as anger or displeasure.

Such stepparents cannot relate to the children as real people because they deny or hold back their true thoughts and feelings. Instead, they overreact. They yell at their own children more strongly than the situations call for, or they finally explode at their stepchildren in terrible fury when they can no longer hold back their real thoughts and emotions.

These stepparents forget that even natural parents occasionally dislike their own children's behavior and are annoyed with them. They forget that love takes many years and shared experiences to build, that it does not happen with a single ceremony or signed legal paper. These stepparents also forget that holding back thoughts and feelings allows those feelings to grow stronger and prevents the problems that cause them from being aired, discussed, and resolved. Expecting too much too soon, stepparents receive only their stepchildren's coldness in return. They then feel unappreciated because they try so hard to feel and show love but the children do not return it.

After a time, stepparents who expect too much from their relationship with their stepchildren pull back, feeling guilty and angry with the young people and with themselves. Their unreasonable expectations give them false hopes, disappointments, and frustrations that will begin to stress the new family.

Stepchildren also feel pressure to love their stepparents instantly, but they cannot. These children have lost an important parent through death or divorce. They have been hurt, and they now distrust relationships with adults. They are slow to warm up to a stepparent, especially if they resent the stepparent for replacing them in the natural parent's affection or for trying to become a substitute parent. Young people want to keep their close and loving relationships with both natural parents, and if they believe the stepparent stands in the way of those important bonds, they become very angry.

Other children suffering loss ask too much of a stepparent, demanding that he or she make up for all past hurts. No matter how caring, few stepparents can meet these equally unrealistic ideas.

In either case, instant love is not possible for anyone, and both end up disappointed and frustrated. Both need to realize that differing degrees of love exist. People can like each other a little or a lot, love each other a little, and possibly love each other a lot. Love matures slowly, and stepparents and stepchildren can have good relationships built on goodwill, respect, cooperation, and sharing even if they do not love each other at first.

*Replacement Parents.* Most parents marry again in order to become a family once more. Parent and stepparent assume that the latter will be the children's "new mother" or "new father." They mistakenly believe that the marriage will suddenly change all relationships into the family as it used to be. Sometimes a parent wishes for a new family as a gift for the children. The first parent left through death or divorce, and the natural parent feels responsible for the children's loss and believes remarriage will make it up to them by giving them a new parent. At other times, a parent wants to erase the past and replace the divorced or deceased natural parent in order to prove himself or herself successful at marriage.

Many stepparents also see themselves as replacement parents. They want to come into the home, make up to the children for all past neglect or abuse, and create a new family. Such a stepparent wrongly expects the family to start over again as if from day one. Since this adult is now a "parent," he or she expects to be accepted and to receive the love, affection, loyalty, and obedience due to a natural parent.

Some stepparents even marry in order to become instant parents. Not having married as young as their friends did, the idea of having a ready-made family appeals to them. It means looking like a successful adult and catching up with their friends.

Occasionally, children, too, wish to see their stepparent as a new parent. These children set unrealistic goals for their relationship because they want the stepparent to cherish and love them the way the absent parent did. Some wish for the stepparent to love them the way their own absent parent never could. Young people dream about the way they want their stepparent to act toward them. When these dreams do not come true, they are disappointed and angry and they act out those feelings in annoying ways.

Children already have two natural parents, whether or not both live together in the home. Even deceased parents remain alive in the memory of all but the youngest children. No replacements are possible. Additional parents, however, *are* possible. When a stepparent or child expects the new adult to replace the natural but absent parent in the child's life and heart, both set themselves up for disappointment. No one can take another person's place.

Stepparents can offer friendship, understanding, and kindness to stepchildren. Both can build meaningful and enjoyable bonds over time if they understand and accept the differences between their relationship and that of natural parents and children. It may become the most important relationship either the adult or the young person has ever known. When they set realistic expectations for their relationship and begin gradually to know each other as persons, trust and respect can grow. So can genuine love and affection. Stepparents can become additional parents but never replacement parents to their stepchildren.

Even when the stepparent is more loving, more caring, and more of a "real" parent to the children than the absent mother or father ever was, no one can pretend that the absent natural parent never existed. No one can remove the facts of biology. The place of day-to-day parenthood, however, can be earned by a devoted stepparent. It is more accurate to say that replacement mothers or fathers are not possible, but additional parents are possible.

*Disciplining Stepchildren.* Stepparents enter their new family with varying ideas about the relationship they want with their stepchildren. Some stepparents like the notion of parenting their spouse's children. They feel confident that they can walk in and automatically be "parents." They expect their stepchildren's obedience, cooperation, respect, and love. They expect to know how to handle the young people even though they do not really know them as persons or have had no prior experience as parents to their own children.

Some stepparents do not want to raise other people's children. They see themselves as married to parents but not as parents. They do not want to look after their stepchildren's needs, set and enforce rules, or clean up after the young people. They do not expect to give advice or support. These stepparents simply want to have happy marriages and prefer to keep out of their stepchildren's way. Children are part of the whole package, and these stepparents do not want to become more involved with them than a friendly "Hello" at breakfast.

Other stepparents want to become additional parents to their stepchildren. They know it will not be an easy task. They do not know the young people well, and they do not know the rules under which they lived in their original or single-parent family. These stepparents understand that trust, respect, and obedience take time to grow, but they want to nurture and guide their stepchildren as parents do.

Natural parents also have ideas about discipline and family relationships. Some natural parents want their spouse to set and enforce rules, and the natural parents openly support the stepparent's involvement. Other natural parents have very close relationships with their children born of years of living together, and they feel uneasy about allowing their spouse to take over.

In any case, both adults must frankly discuss what they want from each other as to parenting the young people. They must take time to resolve differing views of child-raising. Should the couple spell out all the rules to each other before telling the children? Should the natural parent set and enforce rules with the stepparent remaining silent until the adults can talk about the matter in private? Should the stepparent speak up quickly and freely when the young person acts in an annoying way? Learning how to go about disciplining children takes time, experience, and testing. The people involved must openly learn what each expects and together decide what role each must play.

When a stepparent wants to be an active parent and the natural parent fully agrees to this goal, they work together to make the arrangement a reality. Stepparent and parent decide what children's behavior is proper and what is not. They decide what limits should be set and what should be done and by whom when children break the rules. The stepparent must assert himself or herself firmly, consistently, and fairly early in the marriage, letting young people know where the limits lie, confronting misbehavior when it occurs, and letting youngsters know when enough is enough. The natural parent should back up the stepparent's actions so that they act as a team. When both adults agree to share parenting roles and act together in firm, fair, and consistent ways, young people test and quickly learn the limits.

When both adults agree on their relationships with the young people regarding discipline and parenting, the family works well because the rules and expectations are clearly defined and firmly enforced. On the other hand, when the stepparent wants to become actively involved with raising the stepchildren but the natural parent does not fully support this goal, the stepparent feels like an outsider, frustrated, angry, and useless. If the stepparent does not want to become active but the natural parent insists that the new spouse take on parental duties, arguments and tensions result. When the adults cannot openly agree about parenting roles, everyone loses. Friction grows among all family members, and everyone, children and adults alike, becomes confused, frustrated, and angry.

*Loving All Children the Same.* Another unrealistic idea that stepparents bring into their new family is that they will love all children—stepchildren and natural children—alike. In attempts to be fair, stepparents pretend all the young people are equal. They believe they must love their stepchildren as much and in the same ways as they love their natural children. Stepparents often feel that they wronged their natural children in their first family and will now even the score by being better parents to their stepchildren. Other stepparents want to make up for their stepchildren's past losses and want to please their new spouse by loving the stepchildren.

In these ways, many parents try to protect their natural children from feeling the loss of their first family. In effect, natural parents tell their children, "You do not miss anything (or anyone) because you still have two parents at home who love you as if they were your natural parents. This new family is just like the old one." Pretending that the stepparents love their stepchildren just as they love their natural children helps keep up this fantasy of no loss.

At other times, stepparents feel guilty because they do not feel deep love for their spouse's children. They try hard not to let their real feelings show, and they act and speak as if they loved their stepchildren. They buy all children in the household the same Christmas gifts regardless of their interests. They set the same bedtime for all children regardless of their ages. They believe that if the same gifts and rules stand for all children, no one will feel treated unfairly and no one will be accused of favoritism.

Stepparents want so much to be fair that they try too hard. They forget that the children are individuals with separate needs, interests, personalities, and abilities. As a result, natural children feel that their parent no longer cares about them or values their special bond. Natural children resent seeing their stepbrothers and sisters treated the same as they are when the newcomers have not earned the parent's special closeness or affection. Stepchildren, on the other hand, resent this fake equality because the stepparent shows no awareness of them as separate individuals.

Again, unrealistic ideas about stepfamily relationships bring trouble and hurt feelings to everyone. Children differ from each other. Relationships between natural parents and children differ biologically and emotionally from those between stepparents and stepchildren. All the pretending in the world will not change those facts. People and relationships are unique.

Not even natural parents in a first family can love or treat all children the same. They can love all their children deeply, but they also love and treat them according to their ages, needs, personalities, and interests. For stepparents to pretend feelings for stepchildren that do not exist does not allow them to build real and lasting ties with them. Pretending love and equality is a lie, and while everyone knows it, no one can deal with it because the real emotions and thoughts remain hidden.

Trust built on honesty, interest, and sincere attempts to know each other as separate individuals brings more satisfying and enduring results. It takes time, testing, and retesting to build real bonds between stepparent and stepchildren. Some stepparents and stepchildren will never love each other. Some will slowly build feelings of trust and affection that may turn into love. Stepparents and stepchildren do not have to love each other in order to have a satisfying relationship. Patience, understanding, and respect will do.

*Becoming a "Real" Family.* Another unrealistic idea of remarried parents involves making their second family into a "real" family. They want their household to feel and look like a "normal" family. Parent, stepparent, and children want to feel close, loving, and happy. They want to be the way "real" families are supposed to be, the way they used to be. The mistaken ideas about instant love, replacement parents, and treating all children alike work toward reaching this end.

Looking like a "real family" sitting together in church or synagogue is important to many stepfamilies. Ted Jones and his new wife showed much concern about the way their stepfamily appeared together in public. Ted thought that if his wife sat next to her daughter and he sat next to his sons in church, all his friends would wonder how well their new family was getting along. Ted wanted to show everybody that his was a successful remarriage and that every member had a good relationship with every other member. To this end, Ted planned ahead who would sit next to whom and who would walk down the aisle with whom. As a rule, he deliberately sat next to his stepdaughter and told his sons to sit next to their stepmother. Ted wished he did not have to "stage" his family's appearance in public, but he wanted the community to know that all was well in his new family.

While this plan sounds fine, it misses the mark. Many forms of families exist. No one right model of family life works for all individuals, and changes in family styles over time prove that. In efforts to have a successful marriage this time, to feel good about themselves, and to regain the community's respect and approval, many parents try to force their ideas and feelings into molds that exist only in their imagination.

In the real world, no such thing as husband, wife, and children living together in perfect love and harmony exists. There is no such thing as the "ideal" family in which the husband earns money, the wife cares for home and children, and young people are obedient and respectful. In the real world, variations exist. Adults share tasks flexibly. Real people have real emotions. Give and take become necessary. This is true for first families, and stepfamilies deserve the same leeway.

Well-meaning but unrealistic ideas about stepfamily relationships create tensions between the stepparent and stepchildren expecting instant love, instant bonds, instant family, and instant obedience. They create tensions between stepparent and spouse expecting instant trust, instant affection, and instant discipline between stepparent and stepchildren. They create tensions between the stepchildren who need reassurance about their natural parent's continued love and their stepparent's understanding of them as separate, unique individuals. These mistaken ideas build frictions that shake the family's chances of becoming a "real" family.

When people have ideas about what they want to happen and the realities disappoint them, they feel hurt, angry, and confused. For a while, they hold back their unhappy emotions, denying that they have any problems. Already experienced at a failed marriage, family members do not want to rock this boat and risk another disaster. Sadly, holding in thoughts and emotions builds even more stress in family relationships. It also prevents members from finding the real issues and resolving them. Expecting from members what is not fair, reasonable, or realistic starts the stepfamily off on the wrong track. They *are* a "real" family; they are not, however, a carbon copy of their first family.

*Living With What Is*

Frequently, a stepfamily begins with unrealistic ideas about how members are supposed to feel and act. Coming together with those preset beliefs sometimes prevents members from dealing with the many realities of stepfamily life.

*A Natural Parent Lives Outside the Home.* Even though a stepfamily gives children and stepchildren a home, stepchildren actually live in two separate households. In cases of divorce, one biological parent is alive and living elsewhere. An absent parent presents a real force for all to consider. Children do not give up loving and thinking about their absent parent simply because they do not see each other daily. In cases of death, the deceased parent remains alive in the memories of all except the youngest children.

Belonging in two homes confuses children. They know where they live but wonder where they belong. When the natural parent and stepparent act as if the absent parent does not exist, children become very upset. Except in cases when the absent parent was violent, abusive, emotionally disturbed, or uncaring, children do not want to stop loving and caring for both natural parents. They do not want to be forced to choose one over the other. In fact, when the natural parent who plans to remarry tells them they will have a "new parent," children fear they will be forced to give up their absent parent. Children can never be forced to give up their natural parent, but they can learn to understand and live with visiting arrangements.

When the adults and children agree on visiting arrangements, they solve one problem of belonging, but they create others. Two homes mean two places to live, two sets of adults with whom to relate, two neighborhoods and sets of friends, two sets of rules and ways of doing things. At first, children feel confused and out of control with all these changes. They wonder where they will put their toys, which clothing belongs to which home, and what behavior is right for each home. Will they be guests in their absent parent's home or will they really be part of the family? Children wonder if their enjoyment and pleasure with one parent will anger the other parent. They experience conflicts of loyalty unless both parents genuinely encourage and support their relationship with the other parent.

Membership in two homes gives children opportunities to belong with both loved parents and to learn different ways of seeing the world. It gives them alternate ways of solving problems. Children gain more experience that helps them grow and mature.

Considering the absent parent is an important reality for stepfamilies, even in what seem like small matters. Who sits where can be a big concern for stepchildren. When they perform in school plays or sports events or receive awards, they often look for a smile or wave from their parents in the audience. They want to be able to rush over afterwards for a hug or praise. When the two natural parents are present but seated apart, children feel a need to choose favorites. For divorced parents to sit apart takes all the fun out of the event for the child who remains loyal and loving toward both.

Ex-spouses must cooperate and show each other courtesy and goodwill in their children's best interests. Given the problems and hurt feelings that led to or stemmed from the divorce, goodwill and good manners may be in short supply. Quite often ex-spouses have strong feelings of anger, hurt, and resentment toward each other. They have put each other through terribly difficult times, and while legal divorce ends their marriage, it does not always end their bad feelings for each other. Not content to spite each other directly, ex-spouses frequently have their children continue their battles. They ask children to give messages to the other parent rather than speaking directly. They tell children bad stories about the other parent, criticizing, lying, or exaggerating the other's faults in efforts to win the children's support. Angry ex-spouses mess up vacation plans, disappoint the children, and force the ex-spouse and stepparent to change their own plans and try to comfort the upset children. Angry ex-spouses question children about the other parent's activities under the pretense of seeing if the ex-spouse is treating the children well. Angry ex-spouses fight in front of their children. They say mean things about the stepparent, secretly afraid the young people will love the new adult more than they love their natural parent. In return, the parent with whom the children live sometimes puts down the absent parent, hoping to make him or her look bad enough in the children's eyes so that they will not want to live with him or her.

The continuing anger and pettiness between their natural parents disturbs young people. The name-calling, blaming, and put-downs make them want to scream with unhappiness and divided loyalties. Dealing with ongoing bitterness between their natural parents stresses children greatly and keeps them from relaxing in their new stepfamily. Meanwhile, the stepparent stands by helplessly, watching his or her new spouse and stepchildren upset, angry, and torn apart.

*Confused Roles.* Recognizing the absent parent's continuing part in the children's lives affects the way the stepparent and stepchildren relate to each other. It raises questions about which adult is really in charge. Does the stepparent or the absent parent set the rules? Does the stepparent or the absent parent have responsibility for the children's daily and long-term well-being? Who should teach children to solve problems? Who should take them camping, to the movies, or out in the street for a game of stickball? Who should teach them to ride two-wheelers or advise them about career plans? Many a stepparent believes he or she must not try to replace the natural parent in the young people's lives, yet the stepparent and stepchildren live in the same household. They cannot help but influence each other. The society and the new spouse expect the stepparent to assist in child-raising and support, yet say the stepparent should not be seen as cruel. Stepparents hear mixed messages about how they are supposed to act with their stepchildren. If they come on too strong, they are accused of trying to take over. If stepparents hold back and let the natural parents discipline the stepchildren, they are accused of not caring about them. Stepparents "look" like fathers or mothers but are not allowed to act as fathers or mothers. Sometimes they find themselves unable to win no matter what they do.

In addition, stepparents sometimes are jealous of their new spouse's continued involvement with the children's absent parent. The cooperation between ex-spouses that helps children disturbs an insecure new spouse. By their presence alone, stepchildren constantly remind a stepparent of the spouse's past intimate relationship with another man or woman. Stepchildren physically look like their absent parent or have similar mannerisms or habits. All are reminders of the absent parent, and a stepparent wonders if the new spouse makes comparisons. Is the stepparent as good at parenting as the absent parent? Is the stepparent as good a lover as the ex-spouse?

Stepparents do not have their new spouse all to themselves because they realize that any marriage that produces children never ends. As a consequence, stepparents are confused about their role as husband or wife or parent.

Stepchildren also make comparisons between their stepparent and their absent parent. The stepparent may not be as considerate, as fine a cook, as neat, as generous, or as flexible as the absent parent. Whether based on true experiences or idealized memories, stepchildren have grounds to compare.

While comparisons are natural, they are also unfair to all concerned. No two people are alike. No two parents or adults or children are alike. Stepchildren wishing to be accepted and respected as individuals should give their stepparent the same chance. Too often, stepchildren use natural differences between adults as unfavorable comparisons between them, and make both themselves and their stepparent angry, hurt, and disappointed.

In other cases, children believe that liking a stepparent means betraying their absent parent. They look for ways to prove their loyalty and love for the absent parent. They do not give the stepparent a chance to be him or herself or let the relationship define its own terms. Unfavorable comparisons between a stepparent and an absent parent give children chances to show their loyalty to the absent parent by giving the stepparent a hard time.

In addition, the relationship between stepparent and stepchildren may be confusing in itself. Their relationship has changed since they first met. While the stepparent dated the children's natural parent, the new adult tried to win the children's affections, too. This adult brought gifts, acted friendly, had flexible rules about bedtimes and junk food, and made a show of really liking the young people.

Frequently the adult meant these friendly actions. On becoming a stepparent, however, the adult expected to lay down the law. Naturally, the young people feel confused, angry, used, or do not take the stepparent's requests seriously. Is this person my friend or just another bossy parent?

Other stepparents never really felt loving toward their future spouse's children, but only pretended to be warm and interested in an attempt to win points with the children's parent. If the children like me, the future stepparent reasoned, so will their parent. When the stepparent's true thoughts and emotions emerge after the wedding, young people are shocked and furious at the trick the stepparent played at their expense. Do we have a close relationship or is this all a lie? Young people resent such two-faced behavior and let their anger show.

What is more, when stepfamily roles become confused and members are unsure who is supposed to do what, children use the unclear situation to their advantage. Aware that their stepparent and natural parent are uncertain how they are supposed to act, young people ask one parent for money and then phone the absent parent to ask for more. Children argue bitterly with the stepparent and then call the absent parent to ask if they can move in with him or her. When a stepparent tries to assert him or herself by setting and enforcing reasonable limits, stepchildren turn and yell, "I don't have to do as you say. You're not my real parent!" Confusion leads to chaos, with nobody cooperating.

Questions about what children and stepparents want or expect from each other remain one of the biggest areas of confusion in remarriage. All express confusion about who sets and keeps the rules, who decides about money, who deserves affection, who deserves to be called "Mom" or "Dad." How much time do members deserve from each other? Who belongs in this family, and do members belong to more than one family? No clear rules exist to guide a stepfamily in answering these questions.

Each stepfamily is unique, and natural differences should guide members' decisions about these issues. For instance, children's age, sex, and situation should determine what roles a stepparent should play. Young children need a caretaker, whereas older children and adolescents need only an interested adult friend. If a stepfamily uses the narrow models of "family" to give it the answers, however, it ignores the realities and makes matters worse.

Stepfamilies achieve the answers through individual and group efforts. Each stepfamily defines its own solutions because the first family's model does not work here. A stepfamily needs time, patience, cooperation, freedom from additional outside pressures, much give and take, and the ability to live for awhile without clear rules and roles. Members need time to accept the changed situation and build relationships that permit flexibility. A stepfamily needs more flexibility than a first family so as to permit ex-spouses to discuss issues about their children. A stepfamily needs flexibility to permit relatives and friends from the first family to keep their ties with stepfamily members if they choose to do so. A stepfamily needs to start with sincere mutual respect and genuine interest in one another, and let their relationships take off from there.

*Trying to Keep Two Families Apart.* Participating fully in two families is difficult for everyone. Parents have as much difficulty with the situation as do their children. Whose rules are in effect in each home? How is one supposed to behave with each family? Whose home does the family visit for Christmas dinner or summer vacation? Who should receive invitations to graduations or birthdays? Unfortunately, not all adults handle these situations well. Some ways of handling the realities of two-family membership can create hard feelings and confusion for all concerned.

John had lived with his new wife, Rita, for the past three years. Her son lived with them. John tried very hard to keep his first wife and his three children, who lived twenty-five miles away, from meeting his second family. He kept photos of his children on his bureau, but he never spoke about them to his new wife or to his stepson. Every other weekend John entertained his natural children at parks, movies, skating rinks, and restaurants. He never brought them into his new home to meet their stepmother or stepbrother. When John's eldest daughter was hospitalized for a serious illness, John visited her daily. He was very upset about her illness but refused to talk about it with his wife or stepson. Rita wanted to help him through this difficult time, but he would not open up to her.

John was a successful lawyer with a fine reputation as a community leader. He had never really failed at anything before and could not accept his part in his failed first marriage. He had been busy finishing law school and building a law practice while his marriage fell apart from neglect. Now he told himself that his two families were better off apart. Bringing the members together was inconvenient and awkward. Why subject anyone to such a ticklish situation as meeting each other when a little planning could prevent uneasy feelings.

The truth was, however, that John preferred to pretend that he had not failed. When he kept his families apart, he could pretend that his life was simple and successful. He dreaded having to face both families at the same time and accept the reality of his failure. At the same time, his first family did not ask to meet his new family, joining in the fantasy that they were still a "real family."

Meanwhile, John's new wife and stepson became concerned about his unusual visiting arrangements. They wondered if he thought they were not good enough to meet his first family. When Rita tried to tell John about her feelings, he would not discuss it. After a few years, Rita's hurt feelings changed into anger. She insisted that John listen to her concerns about his attitude toward her and her son. She insisted that he face reality and show her the public respect and appreciation she deserved. She wanted reassurance that John truly loved her and valued their marriage. John risked losing his second family because he could not accept the loss of his first family.

*Children Feel Pushed Aside by Stepparents*

Remarrying parents feel excited, proud, and happy to find a special relationship with another adult and believe that from now on everything will be great. They expect their lives to be filled and whole again because they have someone they love and can share their life with. Goodbye to loneliness. Goodbye to feeling unattractive. Goodbye to helplessness and failure. Goodbye to making all decisions by themselves.

In the joy and bustle of preparing for their new life, remarrying parents do not see their children's doubts or sadness about the event. Even children who look forward to their new family soon feel as if they are losing once more. Through remarriage, young people feel as if they are losing another parent.

In a way, children do lose something when their parent remarries. They lose the special closeness, the special place, and the special jobs they had during their time as a single-parent family. They lose the long personal talks with the parent about where their lives are going and how they will solve their problems together. Some children slept in the single parent's bedroom so that neither would be lonely at night. With remarriage, children lose the companionship they shared with the single parent when they had to rely only on each other. Children lose the "man of the house" or "little housekeeper" status they held when they took out the garbage, mowed the lawn, dusted the house, or prepared dinner. In their single-parent family, so many jobs to be done meant that everyone played an important part. Everyone needed everyone else's help, and young people were proud of their efforts to support the family. They felt valued and appreciated by their single parent. They and the single parent experienced a wonderful closeness in spite of the many pressures upon them.

Remarriage changes this. The new couple focus their affection and attention on each other and take on many household tasks that the children used to have. Many young people are glad to be rid of the extra chores but are sad about losing their special place in the family. They move back into their own room. They feel pushed aside emotionally and physically. They see their stepparent as a rival for the natural parent's love and are jealous of his or her place in the family.

After months or years of specialness to their single parent, children in the early days of remarriage no longer know where they stand.

Mel, age nine, was one such youngster. He was very upset, and his mother did not seem to care. All she wanted to do was hang all over his stepdad. When the adults went out to dinner Friday evenings, they left Mel with a sitter. When they talked to each other in the TV room, they acted as if Mel were invisible.

Mel and his Mom had been so close during the two years following the divorce. He had learned to set the table and make salads. He never forgot to take the garbage cans to the curb on Tuesdays and Fridays. He learned to scramble and fry eggs for their breakfast. He even stopped playing sandlot baseball in order to keep Mom company.

Now none of that seemed to matter. To his Mom and stepfather, Mel was just a nuisance. On top of this, Mom expected Mel to love his stepfather and treat him the way he would treat his real father. "How could she do this to me," he cried. "We are a real family again," his mother said, but Mel had never felt more lonely in his life.

Feeling left out is natural. Newlyweds need privacy and time alone together to know each other better, to share intimacy. A remarried parent wants to go out to dinner with the new spouse. The couple want to go away for weekends by themselves. They want to spend time in the bedroom with the door locked. They need these chances to build a solid relationship and a solid marriage. A remarried parent does not intend to shut out the children, but these newlywed behaviors make young people feel shut out of the special relationship with their parent.

When young people wonder where they fit into their new family and fear they are no longer important, their resentment and worry lead to angry behavior. Children argue and fuss to get their parent's attention; even annoyed attention is better than no attention. Children start quarrels with the stepparent to see whose side the natural parent takes. Unhappy, confused, and insecure children act rudely and uncooperatively to see how the parent reacts and to tell the parent, "Don't forget me! I'm still here!"

A newlywed parent wants a honeymoon of enjoyable time in the new family but may find only a household turned upside down by frightened and angry children. This behavior shocks the natural parent. What happened to the lovely, helpful, mature young people who helped the parent survive the most difficult times of their lives? What happened to the eager children who really seemed to like the new spouse before the wedding but suddenly are at the stepparent's throat? When the parent does not understand the children's fears about belonging in the new family and does not recognize their worries about the parent's love for them, he or she feels let down and betrayed. The remarried parent stands in the middle between angry young people and an increasingly upset spouse. Put on the hot seat, the parent feels unfairly forced to choose between the children and the new mate. If he or she gives in to the children's unreasonable yet understandable behavior, the spouse becomes upset. If he or she sides with the spouse in an effort to keep the marriage on track, the young people's worst fears are confirmed; they are even more frightened, grow more angry, and act worse. The problems multiply.

Grace and her son, Chad, age eight, had lived together in a single-parent family since Chad was a toddler. Making a new life together had not been easy, but Grace and Chad both worked at their own levels to keep their small family going. Grace worked full time as a physical therapist, and Chad took responsibility for putting his soiled clothes in the hamper each night, setting the table, and picking up his toys. The two spent evenings and weekends playing, talking, and growing very close.

When Grace remarried five years later, Chad changed from a friendly, helpful boy into a rude and uncooperative youngster when his stepfather, Bruce, was around. Chad did not like Bruce's getting so much of Grace's attention. Grace sat next to Bruce on the sofa while they watched TV; she used to sit next to Chad. She talked mainly with Bruce over the dinner table; she used to focus only on

Chad. Grace and Bruce sometimes visited their adult friends and left Chad at home with a sitter. Chad had liked Bruce all right before the wedding, but he did not like waiting for supper until Bruce came home. He did not like the fancier meals his Mom cooked for Bruce. He did not like his Mom's and Bruce's bedroom door locked on Saturday mornings.

One day, Chad had enough of feeling left out and less important to Grace than he used to be. He missed the bologna sandwiches, tacos, cheeseburgers, and macaroni and cheese he and Mom used to eat.

"Why do you always cook what he wants?" Chad yelled at Grace. "I hate this food," he cried, "and I hate you!" he screamed at Bruce and ran out of the room.

Grace sat stunned. She was shocked and embarrassed at what Chad had said, and she was torn between pleasing her son and her new husband. Bruce also sat silently. The lecture about balanced and nutritious meals would not work now. Chad was hurting, and both adults knew it.

After dinner, Grace and Bruce talked frankly about how Chad had behaved and why the boy felt so unhappy. It was not simply the favorite foods that Chad missed; he missed the special closeness he had shared with his mother before Bruce arrived. The adults decided that Chad deserved some "special time" alone with Grace. Since Bruce bowled with his office league on Wednesday nights, that would be the night Grace and Chad would have as "theirs" to spend as Chad wished.

At breakfast the next morning, Grace explained the idea to Chad, and he was excited. Having every Wednesday evening alone with his Mom to shop, play video games, or eat in restaurants Chad liked sounded great. After a few months of Wednesday "dates with Mom," Chad started wearing his best clothes for the occasion. He and Grace spent days discussing how they would spend their hours together. It became the highlight of Chad's week. Everyone enjoyed the new arrangement, and Chad stopped feeling angry at Bruce. Each man in Grace's life knew he had an important place with her.

When a parent remarries, the couple's new relationship forces a painful but healthy separation between the natural parent and the children. Drawn close during their single-parent days, parents and young people nevertheless have separate lives to live. The young people's sense of loss after remarriage is real, however, and the adults must respond with understanding, patience, fairness, and reassurance. Most young people get used to their stepfamily's limits and relationships if reassured of the parent's continued love and interest. They need some time alone with the natural parent to feel wanted and valued. They need to see the parent able to love both them and the new spouse in different ways. Over time, happy remarriage usually makes everyone in the household happier. For the first few months, however, a stepfamily feels much stress and each member seeks to feel part of the whole.

*Remembering Their First Loss.* Children of remarriage lost their first family. Divorce or death broke their trust in adult relationships and in the world's safety and predictability. Children feel that if people really loved each other, they would not leave. It takes a long time for many young people to let themselves become close to other adults. The risk of disappointment and hurt is too great. For that reason, as well as for others mentioned earlier, the instant love expected by many stepparents and children becomes impossible.

In addition, most young people in the United States grow up with only two adults in their home on whom to depend. They rarely have grandparents, aunts, uncles, or cousins intimately involved with their daily lives. Young people, therefore, look to their natural parents to meet all their emotional and physical needs. That is what they are used to. Their security and sense of self rest with their natural parents alone. As a result, young people in general are not able to trust other adults, even when those adults call themselves stepparents.

To young people, a stepparent stands for their loss. A stepparent's presence in the home reminds them of the death or divorce that made the absent parent leave. Children look at the stepparent and remember the way life used to be. They look at the stepparent and remember the loss of the special place with their natural parent in a single-parent family. Children feel the loss, too, of their dreams of putting their first family back together. They believe the parent's remarriage betrays the absent parent. They see in the stepparent the loss of the "givens" that told them who they were and where they belonged. Young people feel additional loss when they move from their old home, leave an old school, and leave old friends. Stepchildren experience many losses at which their parent and stepparent do not even guess. These young people need time to mourn all over again at the very time when the remarried parent and the stepparent expect them to feel glad about their new family. Young people need time and opportunity to grieve for their lost family, lost hopes, and lost loves. They need time to let go of these important things through sadness, anger, and even depression if they are ever to become free to grow close to their new family, build other hopes, and care about other people.

For many young people, on the other hand, remarriage begins a happy time. Their first family was a troubled, sad place if their parents fought much of the time or if one parent was violent and abusive to the children. A stepparent may bring warmth, caring, and an orderly family life. Remarriage for these children is a time of new hope for a satisfying family life. They are the lucky ones.

For many, grief hurts so much that they use anger instead of sadness to feel in control. Some young people pretend not to care about their losses because the sadness of caring hurts too much. It is easy for parents and stepparents to miss the clues that signal children's mourning because the adults do not expect young people to feel that way about an event that makes the adults so happy. Problems arise when adults misread the sadness, anger, or "I don't care" attitudes to mean disapproval of them or their new marriage. These are important feelings if the young people are one day to let go of the past and be free to truly enter their stepfamily.

*Feeling Torn Apart.* Stepchildren already have two natural parents whom they love. A stepparent can become an additional parent or a concerned adult friend, but not a replacement or substitute parent. Children told to react to a stepparent as if to a natural parent respond with anger, guilt, hostility, rebellion, or pulling away instead of with the love and obedience that the adults want. Most children do not want to give up a bond with the absent parent no matter how difficult the relationship is. Asking them to deny or forget this important tie tears young people apart.

Even when a stepparent is kind, interested, and caring, young people feel divided loyalties. Redecorating a home seems to children as if the stepparent were trying to get rid of the absent parent's personality or influence in their lives. Young people view any change in furniture, wallpaper, or appliances as criticism of their absent parent.

Nevertheless, a stepparent fixes tasty and regular meals, makes the home neat and beautiful, gives attention and affection to the natural parent and the stepchildren, helps with homework, and sets fair rules and limits. A stepparent may be everything the new family could hope for, but young people still feel upset. They resent a stepparent who tries to be better than their absent parent. No matter how well-meaning the stepparent, young people sometimes perceive his or her behavior as a put-down of their absent parent. Other children suspect that the stepparent's actions are too good to be true and just intended to buy their affection.

Distrusting a stepparent is a natural first reaction. Ben, age twelve, was upset with himself, but he believed he had acted the way he had to. Visiting his Dad and stepmother was a mixed bag for him. He loved Dad, and the two did all sorts of neat things together. Sailing, movies, or even washing the car felt great.

The problem was his stepmother. She was younger and prettier than Mom, and she made Dad happy. She always seemed glad to see Ben, and bought a dresser for the guest room just for Ben's clothes and games. She left him alone with Dad and did not try to butt in where she was not wanted.

The problem was simply that she was not a problem. Ben wanted to hate her because Dad had known her before he divorced Mom. Mother still acted angry about her and said mean things about the way she had broken up their first family. The last time Ben had returned from visiting his Dad, he had told Mom about the new dresser. Mom looked furious and walked away.

Ben wanted to like his stepmother but did not want to upset his mother, so he decided to be rude to his stepmother and told her the dresser was ugly. Ben felt bad when his stepmother looked so hurt, but he told himself he had to do it this way.

Sometimes young people want to dislike their stepparent in order to remain true to their absent or custodial parent. Children believe they have only a certain amount of love to give; if they give it to a stepparent, they will have less love to give their natural parent.

When they find themselves feeling good about the stepparent, therefore, some young people feel guilty and disloyal to their natural parent. They are afraid that if they let themselves like the stepparent, their natural parent will stop loving them. Liking a stepparent puts many young people in a difficult spot. To make themselves feel less guilty or disloyal, stepchildren sometimes act as if they do not care about a stepparent's thoughtfulness. They are angry and act rudely instead of showing how happy and grateful they really are. These young people do not realize that they can truly love both adults without taking anything away from either one.

Unless a stepparent understands the stepchildren's dilemma, he or she feels hurt, unappreciated, and resentful. He or she often pulls away from building satisfying bonds with the stepchildren, believing they do not like him or her. Acting like an adult friend rather than a replacement parent, an additional parent rather than a substitute parent, the stepparent stands a better chance of winning the stepchildren's acceptance.

*New Rules and Routines.* Stepfamilies face changed rules and routines as a new person with individual ways of doing things enters the household. A stepparent sometimes expects different things and acts in different ways than the absent parent. One cooks gourmet meals that take hours to prepare whereas the other believes in grilling fast hamburgers or hot dogs. One defrosts frozen vegetables, the other prepares only fresh vegetables. One expects young people to ask permission before opening the refrigerator door for a snack; the other believes young people should have free run of the kitchen as long as they clean up after themselves. Stepparents and absent parents have different rules for watching TV, for finishing homework, for the number of baths young people need each week. One washes clothes only when the washing machine is full; the other washes three times a week no matter what. One thinks family members should make birthday gifts by hand; the other buys gifts at the store. One prefers plastic Christmas trees; the other wants only fresh Scotch Pine. All these and more differences mean changes to which young people must adjust.

The mood at home also changes. One adult's personality is warm, open, and friendly; the other is quiet and finds it hard to show affection. One yells; the other whispers. One is easygoing and calm; the other gets upset over nothing. One wants children to speak their minds; the other believes they should be seen and not heard. These differences create a new atmosphere in a stepfamily. One way is not necessarily better than the other; it merely reflects different values, preferences, and tastes.

Nevertheless, these differences cause tensions at first because home does not feel the same. Older children used to handling events in certain ways over the years sometimes feel upset if their stepparent does not do things the same as their absent parent. Young people still wish their lives were the way they used to be and try to defend their absent parent by complaining about the new family's style. They do not want to lose any more of their familiar life than they already have lost. Different ways seem like worse ways.

In addition, changing the manner of doing things affects the way young people see themselves. The old style tells them who they are, and they do not want to let go of any more of their old selves. The changes, therefore, set the stage for clashes between children and stepparent. Both sides need to develop understanding and appreciation of each other's differences. They need to talk out the problems and find ways of living together on which all can agree.

*Mixed Feelings.* Young people react to their single parent's remarriage with mixed feelings. Glad their parent is happy again, they also resent being pushed out of their special places with the parent. Glad to be rid of many household chores, they also miss proving their value to their parent. Young people miss feeling needed and important. They are pleased to have extra time for themselves and their friends, but they also wish they could have more time with their parent again. Similarly, young people enjoy a stepparent's interest, help, and companionship but at the same time are angry at him or her for taking away their special closeness with the parent or for making the absent parent look bad by comparison.

Feeling two ways at once confuses all family members. One minute young people sit on the stepparent's lap and the next moment say something hurtful and unkind. One minute young people cooperate with the new family's rules and the next they complain, "That is not the way my real Dad/Mom used to do it!" These young people fight with themselves as much as with their stepparent. Feeling one emotion about the situation would be more comfortable.

In any case, these mixed emotions represent the young people's positive moves toward accepting their stepfamily. At least now they do not feel angry or sad about *everything*. In the meantime, until they settle down and feel at ease in their new family, adults' patience and understanding of these conflicting signals helps.

*Problems With Money*. Stepfamilies often have money problems. A stepfather frequently works to pay bills for two families, the new one and the first one. A stepfather has legal and moral obligations to meet these financial responsibilities. Paychecks, therefore, do not stretch as far as they otherwise might. Budget-watching and corner-cutting become serious family concerns. Child-support checks from the absent parent arrive on time and in full or irregularly and less than expected. As if stepfamilies were not stressed enough already, money matters bring additional stress.

In addition to the practical need to plan expenses and pay bills, money matters also create emotional stresses. Supporting two families, stepfathers see a declining living standard in each and feel embarrassed and angry that they cannot successfully provide for their families. If they cannot buy that new car, fix the washing machine, or afford new clothing for the children's return to school, stepfathers feel like failures. They are not doing what they are supposed to be able to do as "good husbands and fathers."

New wives resent stepfathers' paying "their" money to some other woman and children to whom the new wives feel no obligation. New wives understand the situation, but it annoys and frustrates them. Angry and upset parents and stepparents show less patience and understanding toward angry and upset children. Economic strains place added burdens on all family members and on their already tense relationships.

*Grandparents' Role in Single-Parent Families*

When families separate and divorce, grandparents sometimes step in and play an important role. Especially when they live nearby, children and even their single parent may move in with the grandparents for a time while the parent begins school or work. The grandparents' home is a stable and safe place while all else is falling apart and new ways of single-parent living have yet to develop. Meals appear on time, clothes are washed and put away, and an adult can look after the children while the single parent is working or dating. Grandparents pay the rent, phone bill, and grocery tab. With self-confidence gone, single parents look to their own parents to help them feel better about themselves and make decisions about how to conduct their new life.

Both children and grandchildren see grandparents as nurturing caretakers, and they occasionally grow dependent on the elderly relatives for advice and financial and emotional support. Even if they don't all live in the same home, frequent visits and phone calls are usual events.

Dependence on grandparents gives the elderly couple much influence in the single-parent family. Since the grandparents pay the bills and shelter the adult and children, they feel they have the right to set household rules and give advice. They may be more strict about bedtime, homework, and chores than the natural parents. Some want a say in what jobs the single parent takes and which dates are suitable.

While allowing grandparents to take charge feels good at first, a welcome relief from the daily problems of living in a new single-parent family, the situation can become a problem in itself. When parent and grandparents disagree about rules or child-raising issues, the young people do not know whose rules to follow. If they obey grandfather, their mother becomes angry. If they obey their father, their grandmother who takes care of them becomes upset. Children wonder how they can confidently take their single parent's advice when he or she appears unable even to look after himself or herself. The situation is confusing and disturbing to young people as well as to the parent.

Likewise, even though the single parents want time out from the problems of adulthood and parenthood, they resent their own parents treating them like children. They left home years before as independent, mature people but now return home shaken and uncertain, wanting guidance and support even as they resent receiving it.

At times, grandparents find themselves caught in the middle.

Although they love their own child and want to be loyal, they see that child as to blame for the divorce. Some believe that their child's selfishness caused the divorce, and they give their daughter-in-law or son-in-law moral and financial support. Having to take sides but not being able to choose their own kin puts grandparents in a difficult position.

Grandparents also find themselves in the middle when their divorced children have their own children for "visits." Some parents do not want to spend time with their children, although they know it is their duty. After a while, the choices for a weekend's fun grow stale, and the parent takes the children to spend time with grandparents.

Children feel cheated out of their special time with their absent parent. From the adult's behavior, they can only conclude that the parent does not want their company. Confused and hurt, they direct their anger toward their grandparents. Similarly, "dumping" children can upset grandparents, who enjoy seeing their grandchildren but believe they should be spending this time with their parent. The grandparents also consider it unfair for the children to be angry with them, whose only fault is trying to help.

In addition, grandparents have their own lives to lead, and not all want to become active parents again. They may not have the interest, money, or energy to be caretakers for their energetic, unhappy grandchildren or children.

Finally, although temporarily moving in with parents or calling them daily for advice or comfort looks like a solution to many a newly single parent's problems, it does not permit the single parent's family to develop a workable arrangement on their own. No mattter how much they want to escape, single parents cannot give up responsibility for their own or their children's lives. Sooner or later they have to learn to take care of themselves, to take care of their children, to make effective decisions.

*Living with Joint Custody*

Many times, law courts give parents joint custody of their children. That means that both parents have legal responsibility to work together to raise their children. At least thirty-three states now require joint custody as either a choice in a divorce settlement in which both parents want legal custody, or as the best choice. Children usually live with one parent and spend weekends and long holidays with the other parent. The parents talk regularly to make decisions about school, medical needs, and other issues that affect their children.

Joint physical custody is also becoming popular. In this arrangement, the children live part of the time with each parent. In each home they have their own bed, clothing, toys, and other personal things that make them feel at home. Parents of school-age children may live in the same school district so that the children can go to the same school and keep their friends.

Although joint physical custody seems like a way to keep children and divorced parents together, several studies now suggest that it does not improve children's adjustment after divorce. Moving from one home to another each week or month is confusing. Children miss the familiar routines of one home. They miss their favorite things, and they miss their neighborhood friends. Sometimes they even change schools weekly. One research study found that these children were more depressed and withdrawn immediately after the divorce than were children living with one parent most of the time, and were more likely to fight with other children and adults two to three years later.

Nor does joint physical custody seem to help the parents' adjustment after the divorce. Angry parents are forced to deal with each other more often, and their regular contact may actually add to the children's suffering. In addition, changing life-styles every week or so is confusing to adults, who now need to make plans for carpooling and child care.

Children under age five need the security of one familiar place and a predictable routine. Teens need one home base for their increasingly active social lives. Both of these groups of children are least likely to gain from joint physical custody. Finally, it seems that parents' attitudes and behaviors toward each other matter more than custody plans in helping both parents and children get used to living happily after the divorce.

# CHAPTER V

## Living with a Stepparent

Children have a different relationship with a stepparent from the one they have with their natural parents. Children and natural parents spend years together, sharing their lives, joys, and troubles. They form habits together and have common, familiar ways of doing things. Children and natural parents know each other as whole people. They know each others' good points and bad points. They come to a stepfamily with a backlog of happy times, shared troubles, support, mutual caring, and confidence. No matter how kind and interested, a stepparent is still a stranger to these children. They hardly know each other, let alone trust or love each other. That is the reality.

What is more, not all stepparents are alike. Not all children are alike. Not all situations are alike. While stepparents bring certain general problems into their new family, each stepfamily finds its own differences and creates its own solutions.

### Living with a Stepmother

Stepmothers come in different forms:

1. A stepmother who lives with her husband and his children.
2. A stepmother who lives with her husband, and his children visit on weekends and holidays or on some other schedule.
3. A stepmother who lives with her children, her husband, and his children.
4. A stepmother who lives with her husband and his children, and her children visit on weekends and holidays or on some other schedule.

5. A stepmother who lives with her husband, her children and his children visit on weekends and holidays or on some other schedule.

*What Stepmothers Expect.* In many cases, stepmothers live with their stepchildren and deal with them closely as part of their daily routine. Stepmothers run the home, help the children buy clothing, prepare meals, and influence the rules for watching TV, doing chores, attending school, and going to church. Our society says mothers are supposed to do these things. Mothers are supposed to tend to the family's emotional life by comforting, advising, and supporting family members. They are supposed to keep the family functioning smoothly and calmly, to create a happy home life. Stepmothers accept those roles, too. In fact, our society expects stepmothers to work harder than stepfathers to make remarried families succeed and feel like "real" families. Stepmothers are put under much pressure to make the family "work."

Our society also tells stepmothers not to be wicked and cruel like fairytale stepmothers. Our culture tells us to watch out for stepmothers and pictures them as selfish, cunning women looking totally after their own interests at the expense of their stepchildren's needs.

Natural mothers use the wicked stepmother stories to frighten children into obedience. They tell the children to appreciate their mother because if she leaves or dies, no cruel stepmother will ever love them or care for them as well as she does. Relatives and neighbors use the stepmother tales to tell stepchildren, "She's not your real mother," or "She cannot love you like your real mother," in attempts to make the children remain loyal to their absent parent.

The many fears and suspicions that come with the title stepmother unfairly create problems without giving the real person wearing the title a chance to be herself and build her own relationship with the stepchildren. Given this dilemma, the stepmother starts out in a no-win position. Society places on her the burden for making the new family work while at the same time taking away the good will and emotionally positive words that could help her succeed. If the new family builds satisfying relationships, all is well. If it fails, the stepmother often receives the blame.

*Why Stepmothers Marry Men With Children.* Stepmothers marry men with children for many reasons and with many different expectations.

Some stepmothers want to become part of a new family. They want to love their stepchildren and help them grow into maturity. These stepmothers enjoy the caring role that keeps a family with children a satisfying place to live. They expect to build relationships with their stepchildren gradually as they come to know, understand, and trust one another. This is a good attitude with which to start a stepfamily.

Some stepmothers marry men with children because loving the children's father makes them feel good about themselves, makes them feel attractive, valuable, and desirable. Like it or not, the stepchildren come as part of the deal. The situation allows no trade-offs. These women want love and attention for themselves. They do not want to parent another woman's children. If never married before, these stepmothers expect their husband to give them as much attention as if they were a couple without children. They resent the stepchildren's involvement with their father because it means less of his time and affection for themselves. These stepchildren sense that they are in the way and resent their stepmother's treating them as so much extra baggage.

Other stepmothers marry men with children because they want the children, the husband, and the community to love, respect, and admire their parenting efforts. They want to make up for all the bad things the children's natural mother did. They will cook better, keep house better, treat their stepchildren better, and love their new husbands better than did the first mother and wife. These stepmothers expect to make up for everyone's past hurts caused by death or divorce, create a close-knit, happy, "real" family, and be living proof that not all stepmothers are wicked or cruel. They expect their stepchildren to accept them as parent at once and to love them instantly. They expect appreciation and admiration. These stepmothers try to please everyone with their winning virtues but usually end up pleasing no one.

Whatever the reasons for marrying a man with children, stepmothers quickly see that they must develop good bonds with their husband's children in order to have a happy marriage. If stepmothers and their stepchildren openly or secretly hate each other, the women risk losing their husband's love and they risk failing at marriage. If stepmothers tell their husband about problems they are having with his children, the husband may start thinking of his new wife as a bad mother and lose respect for her.

*Stepmothers and Stepchildren at the Start.* In the beginning, a stepmother faces difficulties with stepchildren. Stepchildren resent their stepmother's taking the love that rightly belongs to their natural mother. The stepparent stands for the loss of their first family, of their absent parent, of their dreams of reuniting their parents, of their special bond with their single parent. Some stepchildren feel torn between two adults; they believe loving or even liking the stepparent means betraying their natural parent. If children care about their stepparent, their natural parent might stop loving them. What is more, the loss of their first family makes young people lose trust in relationships with adults. All these issues mean that stepchildren do not usually welcome their stepmother into the new family.

*Factors That Make Life Easier for Stepmothers.* In certain situations, stepmothers have fewer problems than in others. If stepmothers live with their natural children as well as with stepchildren, they tend to have better relationships with the stepchildren than if their own children live with the father or grandparents. Living with and caring for stepchildren while unable to do the same things for their own children makes stepmothers feel guilty. As many stresses as children and stepchildren create, stepmothers are more willing to work out the conflicts if their natural children live with them.

Age also plays an important role in how stepmothers and stepchildren relate. Younger children tend to be more trusting and accepting of a stepmother than older children. Babies, for instance, need physical care, comfort, and love. They accept any person who fills these physical and emotional needs. Older children have strong bonds with their absent parent, and they also have their own habits and ways of doing things. Getting used to a stepmother who not only replaces their absent parent but also has different rules and tastes makes life harder for them; loyalty conflicts and old habits become stressful issues.

Moreover, as children approach adolescence, they normally start pulling away from the family and often criticize and argue as a way to start the separation process. These young people are less likely to have friendly relationships with their own parents, let alone with a stepparent whom they feel extra reasons to dislike.

Flexibility works two ways, and younger stepmothers frequently have better relations with their stepchildren than do older stepmothers. The younger the stepmother, the fewer life-style patterns she has to change. What is more, younger stepmothers often have younger, more flexible stepchildren, willing to give the stepmother a chance.

Another factor that can make life in a stepfamily easier for a stepmother involves the way she sees herself acting in the new family. A stepmother who expects to be a replacement or substitute mother to the stepchildren quickly meets their resentment and resistance. They already have a "real" mother, and the absent mother remains important in their thoughts and actions. Instead, if a stepmother sees herself as a sincerely interested, caring friend or as an additional parent to her stepchildren, she can give them all the interest, affection, and support she has to offer. This stepmother does not try to replace or compete with the children's absent mother, and she allows the relationship with the stepchildren to build slowly and naturally.

This approach gives the stepchildren room to belong to two households without feeling disloyal to either. It allows older children and adolescents who need less mothering to build relationships with the stepmother based on separateness and independence on one hand and shared interests and affection on the other.

*Issues That Create Problems for Stepmothers.* Stepmothers make problems for themselves when they have unrealistic ideas about their role. Expecting to feel instant love for stepchildren and to receive instant love and obedience in return leads to disappointment. Expecting to make up to the children for all their past hurts and neglect means disappointment. Expecting to make the household into a big, happy family just like a first family also means disappointment. Trying to be a replacement parent means disappointment. Wanting a great deal of attention, affection, and privacy with their new husband means disappointment.

Stepmothers start their new marriage hoping for so much and trying so hard. Yet, they often face in return stepchildren's coldness, anger, arguments, and tears and their new husband's scolding looks or critical words about not handling the home situation well.

Stepmothers find themselves competing with the children's absent mother. By their presence alone, stepchildren remind stepmothers about their husband's first wife, whom he once loved and with whom he had children. Knowing that they now have their husband's love, many stepmothers still are jealous of the affection and ties their husband shared with his first wife. They suspect that their stepchildren and husband compare them to the absent mother. Stepmothers desperately want to win this secret contest.

Stepmothers who feel unsure of their value and importance in comparison to a first wife need to prove themselves better wives and better parents. They need to prove they are not homewreckers or wicked women. A few even forbid their stepchildren to call them "stepmother" or tell them, "You're not my real mother!" Every reference to their first family or absent mother makes insecure stepmothers uneasy.

In addition, stepmothers often dislike many of the realities of the stepfamily situation. They sometimes resent splitting the husband's salary between two families. They dislike having to cope with uncooperative, ill-mannered, unhappy stepchildren. Stepmothers did not create the children's problems, but they still have to help solve them.

In other homes, stepmothers are angry when visiting stepchildren completely ignore them. They feel the young people's coldness as saying, "You are nothing to us. You do not exist or matter at all." Dealing with these and other upsetting realities puts many disappointed stepmothers into a sour mood. All they wanted was to be part of a satisfying marriage and a happy family, but what they have is a house full of problems.

*Mealtime Problems.* Stepmothers also have direct conflicts with stepchildren, and problems begun elsewhere often appear at mealtimes.

Mealtimes set the scene for upsetting clashes between stepmothers and stepchildren. Children are used to eating certain foods prepared certain ways. These are matters of habit and personal preference.

Meals also involve matters of identity. Foods fixed in certain ways remind children of life in their first family with both natural parents. Foods remind children of what they remember as the happiest times in their lives, living with both parents. Roast beef brings memories of birthday dinners, and turkey reminds them of Christmases together. Even changing the seating order around the dinner table in a stepfamily upsets young people, who feel more like themselves if they can sit in their "right" places. Sitting in the same order but with new family members included makes stepchildren feel strange. They resent the intruders for making them feel as if this is no longer their family.

Meals, then, reflect both children's tastes and their feelings about themselves and their family. When stepmothers prepare different foods or familiar foods in different ways, stepchildren complain. They find fault with the food because it tastes and looks different from what they are used to, and the difference reminds them of their first family's breakup.

Karen, age ten, had trouble with family meals after her Dad's remarriage. She sat at the dinner table and pushed her lamb stew around the plate with her fork. "This food looks gross!" she complained under her breath but loud enough for her stepmother to hear. "I can't eat this stuff!" Karen pushed her plate away and stared at the tablecloth. This was the third time this week that Karen had come to dinner hungry but refused to eat. She knew her behavior upset her stepmother and angered her Dad, but she did not care. They could make her show up for dinner, make her set the table, and make her sit there, but they were going to have to shove that rotten food down her throat if they wanted her to eat it.

Who needs all this casserole cooking, anyway, Karen thought. Her real Mom used to prepare meals all afternoon, not throw some meat and vegetables into a crockpot before work. Karen liked her real Mom's simple food, not all these weird spices her stepmother used. Besides, if her stepmother really cared about her new family, she would not work full time. She would not have Karen vacuuming the house on weekends. That was mothers' work.

As she sat thinking, Karen's Dad and stepmother looked at each other but said nothing. "Come on, Karen," coaxed her Dad. "This lamb tastes great. Try it." Karen continued to sit, unmoving, thinking about the box of fig bars she had hidden in her bedroom. "At least I won't starve," she told herself.

For many young people, however, stepparents' cooking means eating good food for a change. Experienced cooks and eager to please their new family, many stepparents fix delicious meals. The difference is a welcome change from frozen dinners or a quick and easy sandwich for the evening meal. What is more, sitting down together as a family to eat and visit across the dinner table feels much better than the "every man for himself" attitude in many single-parent families.

To stepmothers, complaints about their cooking seem like attacks on them as people. They feel they are failing to please their stepchildren or keep their husband happy. Many believe that serving delicious, attractive meals is one way to win their stepchildren's and new husband's approval and affection. When, after all their efforts to please, stepmothers hear only nasty comments, they feel hurt. When stepchildren push away their meals, stepmothers feel they are really pushing them away.

Mealtimes also provide a setting for arguments about table manners, dress, and who eats with whom. Stepchildren build their eating habits in their first family, and these habits may differ from what stepmothers want. Elbows on tables, reaching across others for salt, the topics that family members discuss, all vary from one family to another. Stepchildren feel comfortable with their old ways. Stepmothers may not like the young people's old ways because they are either not proper or simply different. Some stepchildren feel comfortable wearing play clothes to the table while stepmothers prefer that they dress more formally. Some stepchildren are used to sitting silently at the table while stepmothers expect family members to talk about school, work, or current events. Other stepchildren are used to eating whenever hungry and then rushing out to play while stepmothers now want the whole family to sit around the table and eat together. Differences in habits and personal styles make room for arguments.

Some stepmothers believe that if stepchildren do not act "properly" at the dinner table, the stepmother is a failure. At the same time, stepchildren consider their old habits normal and proper. They feel comfortable doing things the way they do, and they want to keep the emotional ties to their first family and the sense of who they are. Again, practical and emotional issues linked together bring opportunities for conflict.

*Problems with Discipline.* Discipline represents another area of conflict for stepmothers and stepchildren. All mothers say "No" to children at times. Rules and limits teach young people how to make good decisions or act safely. "No playing with matches!" "No roughhousing in the bathtub!" "Bedtime at 8 p.m." "Homework finished before watching TV or playing!" "If you are going to be late, call home first!" These are things mothers in all types of families say to their children. They are part of a mother's job. Children do not like to hear "No!" It keeps them from doing what they want. Mothers stop young people from acting in certain ways and, in return, children are angry at mothers. That is normal. The problem in stepfamilies concerns who disciplines whom. Should the stepmother tell stepchildren "No" or should their natural father?

Stepmothers have special problems in this area; not only are they closely involved with their stepchildren's lives, but they also have to live down the wicked stepmother image. Some stepmothers believe they must be overly kind and lenient with stepchildren, holding back discipline to win their stepchildren's approval as "good guys." Mothers can freely scold their own children, smack them on the bottom, or simply command, "Do it!" When it comes to correcting the same behavior in stepchildren, however, many stepmothers politely ask them to stop, quietly raise their eyebrows, or try not to notice the actions that upset them. The stepchildren cannot take these requests seriously.

Uncertain discipline does not work. Natural children in stepfamilies complain of favoritism. Stepchildren believe they have more power than their stepmother and secretly laugh at her weakness. Stepmothers feel frustrated, angry, and upset about their own failure to keep stepchildren in line. Unless the stepparent and natural parent work together as a team in disciplining the young people, the stepmother is powerless.

Sometimes stepchildren's bad behavior is a game. For many reasons mentioned earlier in this chapter and in Chapter IV, stepchildren are angry with their stepmother and want to fight her in any way they can. They deliberately act in ways they know will upset the stepmother and dare her to do something about it. Caught in a bind, the stepmother blinks first, and the stepchildren win the round. They feel in control and powerful. Some stepchildren want the stepmother to feel a failure, to feel unimportant to the family. They want to hurt the stepmother as they suspect she has hurt them or their absent parent. If the natural parent does not openly support the stepmother's attempts to fairly discipline the children, the whole stepfamily is in trouble.

Carla, age fourteen, sat in her room pretending to be angry. She could hear her stepmother and Dad arguing about her in the kitchen. Her stepfamily had new rules. Carla was supposed to set the table and clear it after meals. She was supposed to put her soiled laundry into the hamper. She was supposed to help with the little kids. Rules, rules, rules. Carla could not stand them.

At first, Carla had refused to help. When her stepmother "suggested" that Carla start doing her chores, Carla laughed in her face. When Dad finally told her to start helping, Carla did what she had to but no more. Sometimes she forgot.

This morning was an example. Carla had wanted to wear her pink painter's overalls to school, but they were dirty. Carla had dropped them near the washer last week and forgotten about them. Today, she could not find them in her closet. She had asked where they were, and her stepmother said that since the overalls had not been placed in the hamper, they had remained where Carla left them.

Carla had refused to go to school wearing anything but the overalls, and her stepmother had refused to wash them. The school bus came and left while Carla finished her own laundry. She walked the mile to school and arrived late, missing her math test. That evening at dinner, Carla had told Dad she failed her math test because her stepmother kept her at home. Soon Dad and her stepmother were arguing about who was at fault, and they sent Carla to her room as punishment.

"What a joke," thought Carla. "And I didn't even have to clear the table!"

Stepmothers want their new family to work. They want the new family to feel close and loving. They want cooperation and affection from their stepchildren. At first, stepchildren fight closeness and cooperation. They want their first family back again and see the stepmother standing in the way. They challenge, test, and embarrass her. If by the end of the first year of the new family young people are still nasty to the stepmother, she feels, "Forget this!" She is tired, frustrated, and disappointed and pulls away from the stepchildren as much as they pull away from her. Then the relationship grows worse and worse for both sides.

In spite of all the testing and strain from working out new family routines and relationships, most stepmothers keep trying to make the new family succeed. They love their new husband and accept the jobs that come with parenting. They understand the need to develop ties with their stepchildren. Stepmothers believe they have something valuable to offer stepchildren: affection, regular meals and smooth routines, homes in which they can grow into mature and happy young people, and advice about how to act and solve problems. Stepmothers offer good will and reassure children that men and women can live happily together with give and take on both sides in satisfying marriages. Stepmothers sincerely want to be good stepparents.

Time helps stepmothers. A year, two years, or three of living together in a stepfamily lets people really know and understand each other. With time and shared experiences, stepmothers and stepchildren stop relating as strangers. When stepmothers understand stepchildren's special need to keep ongoing ties with their absent parent, to be sad about the loss of their first family, to question their own place and importance in their stepfamily and with their remarried parent, and to trust new adults very slowly, stepmothers build strong, caring relationships with their stepchildren. Not all stepmothers and stepchildren come to love each other, but with kindness, respect, and genuine interest in one another, many build strong and satisfying friendships.

*Living With a Stepfather*

Stepfathers come in different forms:

1. A stepfather who lives with his wife and her children.
2. A stepfather who lives with his wife and her children, and his children visit weekends and holidays or on other schedules.
3. A stepfather who lives with his wife, his children, and her children.

4. A stepfather who lives with his wife, and her children visit weekends and holidays or on other schedules.
5. A stepfather who lives with his wife, his children, and her children visit on weekends and holidays or on other schedules.

Over the years, the stepfather's role has changed. Years ago, when death split more families than divorce, mothers and children needed stepfathers to help run the family farm or business. Stepfathers earned the money or produced the goods that kept the family fed, clothed, and sheltered. In the old days, stepfathers married an attractive or rich widow and either acted as father to her children or ignored them. Either way was legally and socially okay. Other stepfathers married a woman with children to gain extra parenting and housekeeping help for themselves and their own children.

Times changed. Today women play more active roles in business and community life. As women's roles expanded, so did men's roles. Many men now take an active interest in family life and childraising. In fact, many men feel more responsibility to spend time with their second family, do more household chores, and are more involved with their children's lives than they were in their first family. Furthermore, men no longer bring home the only decent paycheck.

*Stepfathers' Legal Position*

As a result, stepfathers' position in stepfamilies remains confused. In many states, stepparents have no legal responsibility to their stepchildren. The law sees children as belonging to their natural parents, particularly the one given custody. Stepparents have no legal rights regarding their stepchildren. Stepfathers cannot, for example, sign consent forms for surgery or sign permission for underage stepchildren to marry. Legally, they cannot even allow underage stepchildren to have their ears pierced. Stepfathers have no legal right to keep loved stepchildren with them if their natural parent, the spouse, dies. Legally, stepfathers and stepchildren remain strangers. They hold social rather than legal relationships.

Stepfathers also have no legal duty to pay for their stepchildren's upbringing. That is the natural father's legal and moral responsibility. Stepchildren have no legal claim on their stepfather's insurance or inheritance unless he clearly writes out these requests in his will. Nevertheless, stepchildren and stepfathers live together, and most stepfathers pay to fix their stepchildren's bikes, buy extra clothing, provide good meals, and live in nice neighborhoods.

*Stepfathers and Money*

Money issues put stepfathers in bad spots. Stepfathers may want to support their wife's children, but they resent spending money on another man's children while the young people stay loyal to their natural father, not to their stepfather. If the stepfathers are themselves divorced and paying their own child support and alimony, they may be paying between one third and one half their salary after taxes to their first family and not have extra money to spend on their new family.

Many stepfathers do not earn enough money to keep everyone happy. Sometimes stepchildren believe that the more money their stepfather spends on them, the more obedience and cooperation they owe the stepfather. Unfortunately, not all stepfathers have enough cash to "buy" their stepchildren's good will.

In addition, society tells men that their role as breadwinner earns them the right to be head of their home. Love, respect, and obedience go the the money-earner. Earning money for their family brings men power, social respect, and self-respect. Providing their family with money for beautiful houses, cars, wardrobes, and extras makes men feel successful and good about themselves. Since stepfathers have no legal obligation to support their stepchildren and perhaps have little extra cash to spend on them, they lose the status, power, and respect that usually come to the man of the house. When their new wife works and also brings home earnings, stepfathers' place grows still less powerful in their own eyes and in their family's eyes.

While the laws move slowly toward recognizing the way people really live, society still largely believes that stepfathers do not matter much. Stepfathers are not complete fathers, and they are not complete husbands. They look like the man of the house, but they do not feel like it. To many, the stepfather's place remains unclear and confusing.

*What Stepfathers Want for Their New Family.* Many stepfathers sense the legal and social confusion about their role in a stepfamily, and that adds to their concerns. Often stepfathers come to a stepfamily from their own failed first marriage and with many bad feelings about themselves. They feel guilty about their past mistakes and about leaving their natural children with two divorced parents. These bad feelings make some stepfathers want to totally forget about their first family and natural children to pretend to themselves that they are not failures. Stepfathers want to be more successful as husband and parent in their second family to erase past failures and feel confident about their ability to make and keep strong relationships with people they love.

Stepfathers want many good things for their new family. Sadly, much of what they want is not realistic. Stepfathers want to be effective as father and breadwinner, but stepchildren still hold important emotional ties with their absent father, who pays child support and greatly influences their ideas, values, and goals. Stepfathers want their second family to be a close-knit group, but in reality they must share their stepchildren and new wife with the absent parent and former mate. They want to be the man of the house, make and enforce the rules, and give stepchildren advice and guidance. They want the power and authority that natural fathers have.

At first, however, their wife has more influence over the young people than stepfathers do. In addition, stepfathers have to permit the absent parent to share in influencing the children, making decisions about their care and upbringing, and paying some of their bills. Stepfathers want this to be *their* family and home, yet the absent parent plays such a large role in stepchildren's lives that stepfathers feel left out and not important in their own family. Stepfathers are outsiders to groups formed long before they arrived on the scene. Wanting so much for their new family, stepfathers face many disappointments because they are not the only important adult male in their stepchildren's and wife's lives.

*Relations Between Stepfathers and Stepchildren.* Stepchildren are not ready to act as if they belong to "one big, happy family." The same issues of loss that stepchildren feel about stepmothers apply to their relations with stepfathers. Stepchildren wonder about their own place in the new family and their own specialness with their natural parent. Stepchildren face the same loyalty problems and the same lack of trust in their relationships with adults. Frequently, even stepchildren who had good relationships with their stepfather before the marriage now start acting angry, rude, resentful, and uncooperative. The fantasy of reuniting their natural parents ends with remarriage. Stepchildren have lost their close relationship with their single parent. Many are afraid to show anger toward their natural parents because they fear losing those parents' love, but stepchildren do not have that concern. If a stepparent becomes angry, stops loving them, or leaves, who cares?

In addition, stepchildren's relationship with a stepfather changes after remarriage. They were pals before, as the adult acted friendly, generous, and interested in an effort to gain their support and win their mother's approval. Now the stepfather wants to be the boss in the family. Stepchildren resent his two-faced behavior and his trying to act as if he were their "real" father by scolding and giving orders. Normal confusion about new family roles and routines upsets children and creates much anger as they must change their habits.

Stepchildren's age often affects their relationship with their stepfather. As a rule, younger stepchildren more eagerly accept a stepfather and build a good relationship with him. Younger children depend more upon staying emotionally and physically close to their mother, and they remain close after remarriage. One study suggests that children under age eight have the easiest time building satisfying ties with a stepfather, especially if the children are girls. Younger children also have fewer important jobs and roles to give up when a stepfather arrives. They were not the "little mother" or "little man of the house" who held a special place in their single parent's life before remarriage. A stepfather takes much of the natural parent's time and affection, but not the special place in the home that older children often hold.

Stepfathers usually have more difficulty with children over eight, who experience the greatest loss, who feel the most divided loyalties, and who generally resent a stepfather's presence in their home. While most older children do not quickly accept a stepfather, and while they test, challenge, and push him, given time and experiences together, most gradually come to know the stepfather as a person and then to respect, trust, and even love him.

*Stepfathers and Discipline.* Stepfathers bring differing ideas about discipline into the family. Many expect to act as a parent to their stepchildren and want to set and enforce rules. They want to have a say about stepchildren's behavior. They want to be able to teach, guide, and if necessary punish stepchildren.

Other stepfathers do not feel they have the right to discipline their wife's children. They say little about it when they think the young people are out of line, taking the attitude that the children trust and respect their mother and are more willing to obey her.

What is more, stepchildren do not want their stepfather telling them what to do or how to act. They bitterly resent this new man who tries to act like their natural father.

Stepchildren resent the affection and time their stepfather receives from their mother. They also have their own habits and ways of doing things and do not want to change for anyone, especially for this intruder. The result is frequent angry clashes between stepfathers and stepchildren.

Mothers also have varying ideas about the stepfather's role in discipline. Many welcome their new husband's involvement with their children. They are tired of trying to raise young people by themselves and readily encourage the stepfather to lend a firm hand. Furthermore, the stepfather's moral support and extra help in setting limits is in addition to his physical help. Stepfathers are usually bigger and stronger than mothers, and some young people behave better for men whom they, literally, cannot push around.

Other mothers prefer to shield their new husband from their children and not have him bothered with their misbehavior. In these situations, mothers act as a buffer between the children and the husband. They do all the scolding, correcting, and punishing and let their husband remain safely out of it.

Then too, other mothers are not sure they want their husband to become involved with discipline for a different reason. These mothers feel protective toward their children. They lived closely with them in a single-parent family and have developed their own ways of doing things together. When a new husband corrects the children, these mothers feel it as an attack. The mothers jump in to defend the young people, saying, "They didn't mean it," or "They're just children. Let them be!" At other times, when the husband metes out punishments to the children, the mothers go behind his back and undo the punishments. These mothers say they want their husband to act as a parent, but their actions say something else.

These mothers want to continue their parenting role as it was during their single-parent days. Correcting children is the natural mother's prerogative. These mothers are not clear about what help they want from their husband regarding child-raising, and they issue conflicting messages to him and to the children. In these cases, mother and stepfather must openly discuss their expectations for parenting responsibilities and come to an agreement. Otherwise, the stepfather who wants to act as parent feels like an outsider in his own home, and the stepchildren become confused.

Confused ideas about discipline let children play the parent against the stepparent. Ethan, age eight, had it made. Having a strict stepfather was not the problem he had thought it would be. When he and his stepfather argued about playing with friends after dinner, Ethan went to his mother and she told him to go outside anyway. When Ethan asked for an advance on his allowance to play video games at the mall, his stepfather lectured him for ten minutes on the need to budget his money better. When Ethan asked his Mom for the money, she slipped him two dollars from her purse and told him not to mention it to his stepfather.

Ethan's Mom told him to obey his stepfather, but Ethan knew she usually took his side when they were alone. "He thinks he's such a hot shot," laughed Ethan of his stepfather. Ethan was glad he and his Mom could be close again, and he felt relieved that he was still special to her. Watching his frustrated stepfather fuss and fume amused Ethan. This stepfamily is not such a bad deal, he thought.

Children naturally want to see how things and people fit together in their new family. They want to test the limits, see which rules still hold and which will bend, and see which adult holds the real power. They also want to test their stepparent's interest and concern for them. Many stepchildren deliberately act up in order to find these answers. Even when they do not feel anger or resentment toward their parent or stepparent, they do what they know is not allowed simply to see what happens.

Confusion and mixed signals about discipline put stepfathers in a bind. If a stepfather wants to discipline the children and believes he has his wife's support, he feels helpless, frustrated, and insulted when his wife jumps in to defend her misbehaving children. She says one thing but does another. When parent and stepparent have not agreed on clear rules for discipline, stepchildren quickly know this and use it to their own advantage. They deliberately misbehave to start the newlyweds arguing with each other and ignoring the young people. They act up to make the stepfather shout at them so they can later feel their mother's protective concern and support. Children shrewdly use the confused discipline situation to separate the couple and become more closely involved with their mother.

In the end, the stepfather feels left out, not knowing where he stands in his own family. At that point, the stepfather pulls away from the stepchildren and the new wife, or he scolds the children even more strongly, trying to make them obey.

*Stepfathers and Their Own Children.* As if the discipline situation were not confused enough, stepfathers' own feelings about their natural children complicate it further. Many stepfathers whose natural children live elsewhere with their ex-wife feel guilty about leaving them and living with someone else's children. They are sad that they cannot give their natural children the love, affection, and enjoyable times together that they would like. To give to stepchildren the attention and care they cannot easily give their natural children greatly upsets them. These stepfathers do not consider it fair to become involved with their stepchildren either for fun or for parenting.

On the other hand, stepfathers who feel guilty about leaving their own children often are stricter with their stepchildren than is needed. Because they cannot influence or control their absent children, they give the available stepchildren a double dose. Therefore, stepfathers with no children of their own may have an easier time relating to their stepchildren.

More and more, natural fathers are seeking and winning custody of their children. Many fathers and children live together while the natural mother lives elsewhere. These fathers can be eager to be good stepfathers, acting fairly and caringly with their stepchildren because they know in their hearts they are good fathers. They do not have to stand far back in order to avoid guilt, or be too strict in order to prove they can be effective parents. For many fathers living with their natural children, stepparenting is easier and more effective than for fathers whose own children live elsewhere.

*Developing Effective Discipline.* When stepfathers and their wives fully and honestly discuss their expectations for discipline, deciding who disciplines the children and how, they give stepchildren one clear set of rules. All children, whether in first families or stepfamilies, test the rules and limits and know what to expect if they break them. The initial testing and arguments occur, of course, but over time the limits become clear. With clear and enforced limits, stepchildren are not able to divide the adults or play one against the other. With clear rules, stepfathers and mothers appreciate each other's help, and this unity strengthens their marriage.

When stepfathers and mothers totally agree about the role the man should play in discipline, they need to remember one more important thing for the arrangement to work. A stepfather is still a stranger to his stepchildren. Young people are more willing to cooperate with a stepfather if they know him as a person and respect, trust, and like him. Children need to know that the stepfather does not see himself as a replacement or substitute parent, but rather as an adult friend or an additional parent. Children need a good relationship with their stepfather if they are to listen and obey the rules. When they know that their mother fully supports his actions, and when they care enough about him to want to please him, children obey their stepfather.

Even if a stepfather can force children to go along with family rules, the children are resentful. They cooperate for the moment but soon look for ways to get what they want. Angry stepchildren want to defy their stepfather and prove that he is not really in charge.

Stepfamilies need gradual shifts in discipline rather than making stepfathers instant rule enforcers. With older children and adolescents, the natural parent should take charge of the children, setting and maintaining the rules, while the stepparent stands back. Over time, doing things together as a family, children learn more about their stepparent as an individual worth knowing and obeying. With younger children, stepparents need to act as part of the parent team from the beginning, with full support from the natural parent.

When children and stepparent become friends, the stepparent can better help the natural parent with discipline. In fact, the older the children, the more they listen only to their natural parent. Older children vigorously fight a stepfather's attempts at setting and enforcing rules; they do not accept his right to tell them what to do.

Megan, age five, had a good situation at home. She had liked her stepfather when he was dating her mother, but she wondered if things would change once they became a family. She knew her stepfather yelled at her when she fussed about his cooking or complained about sitting in the back seat, so she stopped complaining. Her mother was the one who usually scolded her when she was wrong, who told her how to act nicer. Her Mom told her when it was bedtime, when she had to do her homework, and when she had to take her bath. Megan could listen to her Mom because she always had. Megan had a real father who lived nearby, and while she liked her stepdad, she did not want another "father." Luckily for her, her stepdad let Mom tell Megan what to do. He did not pretend he was her "real" father. He and she were simply friends who liked each other, and that was okay with Megan.

*Stepfathers Can Make It Work.* Stepfathers start as outsiders in their new family. While this makes for difficulties at first, it also brings advantages.

If stepfathers failed in their first marriage, they now want to be a better husband and father. They bring enthusiasm and a positive outlook. They are ready to put in the time and energy to show interest and affection for their stepchildren. Because they are strangers, they can get to know the young people gradually through daily contact and shared activities. Stepfathers and stepchildren who do not feel forced to love each other can someday become good, caring friends who know and appreciate each other.

If stepfathers take less responsibility for their older stepchildren's behavior, they can be more relaxed and accepting of the children than if they expected to act as the ruling parent. In this way, stepfathers can stay more fair and objective about their stepchildren than can a natural parent. They can side with the children when the young people are right and become trusted allies when the situation calls for it.

Researchers find stepfathers more likely than stepmothers to develop and keep good relationships with their stepchildren because they usually spend much time away from home at work. They have more time than the mother for talking, playing games, and sharing enjoyable activities with the children and need less time for dressing them, preparing their meals, or picking up their toys. Stepfathers have fewer chances to get on their stepchildren's nerves, and they do not have to face the "wicked" stepparent image.

Over time, most stepchildren come to like and respect their stepfather if he does not try to replace their absent father with demands for loyalty, obedience, and love. A stepfather becomes a trusted friend, ready for closeness, affection, and advice when asked. Although this may not be the way "real" fathers act, sensitive stepfathers play an important role in their new family.

*Conclusion*

Stepmothers and stepfathers both face issues that stand between them and having satisfying ties with other members of their stepfamily.

Stepmothers have to prove to themselves and to everyone else that they are not like the wicked stepmothers in fairy tales. They face a community that dares them to make a success of their marriage yet holds them primarily responsible for making the stepfamily work. Stepmothers start out in a no-win position, and it is to their credit that stepfamilies can work well at all.

Stepfathers are too often the oddball, a stranger in their own home, standing outside the important ties between mother and child. Being a stepfather is confusing, legally and emotionally. Issues of money, respect, obedience, affection, and loyalty enter stepfathers' relationships with their stepchildren. These matters are never easy to solve.

Stepparents need flexibility to accept the importance of their stepchildren's first family in their lives today. Absent parents (and ex-spouses) play starring roles in stepchildren's lives. This is uncomfortable in the short run but for the best long term. Stepparents need to forget the ideas of "instant love" or "replacement parent" and allow their ties with their stepchildren to grow slowly from time spent together and getting to know each other. Stepparents can be concerned, interested, and even loving "additional" parents or adult friends to their stepchildren and build happy stepfamilies.

# CHAPTER VI

## Living with Stepbrothers and Stepsisters

Most young people grow up with brothers and sisters. They help each other mature in many ways. Older children teach younger children how to behave. Little children look up to their older siblings and want to be like them. The older ones use correct table manners and their younger sisters and brothers copy them. Older children ride two-wheelers and younger children watch and learn. Older children speak to younger siblings and the little ones learn from early ages to communicate. Watching older brothers and sisters solve problems, cooperate with parents, and act fairly shows the younger ones how it is done. Sisters and brothers challenge, stimulate, and care for each other.

Brothers and sisters keep each other company, play together, and discuss family problems together. They make each other glad they have someone near their own age to listen to their troubles and help them find answers. Even though they quarrel at times, they learn to share and to compromise. Brothers and sisters feel sure of each other's love.

Sometimes brothers and sisters make problems for each other. They have their own moods, tastes, and habits. They have their own abilities, skills, and interests. They have different experiences in the world and different outlooks about what they want from life and how to get it. With so many differences, arguments result. Two children cannot watch two TV shows at the same time on only one set. They cannot all take showers at the same time. One likes to keep the bedroom neat and the other prefers it messy. One likes lots of beautiful new clothes while the other is content wearing the same jeans with T-shirts all week.

Brothers and sisters are friendly rivals. Sometimes they win. Sometimes they give in. At times their differences annoy each other. At other times, the differences do not matter. When their parents treat them all fairly and allow them to be separate individuals and to work out their own compromises, brothers and sisters learn much about the real world and how to live successfully with other people.

Often remarriage brings new children into their home. Stepsisters and stepbrothers, or stepsibs for short, live full time with their remarried parent or they only visit on weekends, holidays, and vacations. Stepsibs become permanent members of their new household or drift in and out, staying a weekend, two weeks, or several months. Some arrive worried about how they will fit in. Some arrive happy to spend time with their "other" family. Some arrive angry from fights with their custodial parent or upset about a crisis in their own life.

However stepchildren arrive, remarried parents expect all the children now related by marriage to get along with one another. Remarried parents want to make "one big, happy family." Stepsibs relating well to each other becomes part of the plan.

*Feelings Children Have About Their Stepsibs*

Stepsibs start their relationships with a big disadvantage: They did not freely choose each other. They did not choose to live together. They cannot choose to stop relating to each other. Stepsibs are stuck with each other because their separate natural parents are married and living together. Parents have more legal and social control over their own lives than do children, and this fact does not seem fair. Parents can decide to divorce. Parents can decide to move into new houses. Parents can decide to marry persons who are strangers to the young people. Children can make few important decisions. Parents act and children can only make the best of it.

All of a sudden, stepsibs have to share their room, dinner table, and parent's time with a household of strangers. They have no warm-ups, no breaking-in time. Stepsisters and brothers have different family backgrounds, different life-styles, different tastes and habits, and different interests without the shared history of blood ties or long-term good will to make the adjustment easier. They have not had the time together to understand and accept, or at least tolerate, their differences. Stepsibs have different genes, different values, different abilities, different personalities, and yet their remarried parents expect them to be "brothers and sisters" and friends as soon as they unpack. Just like that!

For stepsibs, settling into their new family and building new relationships takes at least a year to set up ways of doing things and begin to feel comfortable with each other. They need to work out who sits where at breakfast, which habits and manners will work well in the new family, and which stepsibs will have meals prepared the ways they like them. Stepsibs must decide how to organize their shared room when one is a neat-freak and the other is a slob. They must decide what to do when one studies in silence while the other wants a blaring stereo. They must work out how to share their space yet keep their privacy.

With so many issues between them emerging and unsettled, stepsibs make beginning a stepfamily life tense and stressful for everyone. At first, their feelings about each other range from hate to friendly-but-distant. Many are angry with each other for intruding on their turf and forcing changes in their life-style. They either avoid talking to one another as much as possible or they argue openly and fiercely. Some are jealous of each other and talk about "your Mom" and "our Dad," trying to judge who is more important in the family and who belongs where. Some stepsibs quickly enjoy each other, glad to have ready-made friends at home. Since everyone and every household differs, each set of stepsibs reacts its own way to this new situation.

## Competition Among Stepsibs

With their family turned upside down, young people wonder about their place and their value in their new family. Will they still be the eldest child with the special respect and treatment that position brings? Will their natural parent still love them the most, or will the parent find one of the newcomers more to his or her liking? Since young people in a stepfamily need to be assured that they remain important and special to their natural parent, and since the arrival of stepsibs means even more changes and uncertainty at home, relations between stepsibs frequently begin with jealousy and competition. The young people test each other and their parent to see how they measure up, which children are "best," and whom their parent and stepparent love most.

Competition begins in many ways. Sometimes stepsibs of the same age and sex feel rivalry with each other. Usually sharing the same room and bathroom because they appear to have so much in common, these stepsibs have too much in common to be comfortable with each other. Frequently in the same classes in school, one earns better grades. If they enjoy the same sports, one plays more skillfully. One has more friends and is more popular. One is more attractive or more able to get what he or she wants. When young people are close in age, rivalry develops even in first families, but the competition in stepfamilies feels worse. The "loser" worries that the natural parent will stop loving him or her because the stepsib is more worthy of affection and attention. When parents and stepparents use one child as an "example" to the other, they encourage the unhealthy competition and make matters worse.

Lisa, age fifteen, had a hard time liking her stepsibs. She could not stand visiting her father and his new family. Her two stepsisters were both in high school in a different town, so at least Lisa did not have to see them every day. One was a cheerleader and on the honor roll; the other was student council secretary and also earned A's. They were so slim and cute that Lisa felt obese whenever they were in the same room. At meals Lisa felt especially embarrassed and pushed her food around the plate to disguise how much she ate. In addition, her stepsisters had boyfriends in and out of the house all weekend. Lisa wished she were invisible.

Lisa herself was a good student, used to making decent grades, but lately she had stopped showing her report cards to her Dad. In no way did Lisa feel equal to her stepsisters. Even though they tried to act friendly, they had nothing in common. Lisa was large and big-boned. She was a good listener and had friends but was by no means popular. They always had something interesting to say to her Dad while Lisa could think of nothing to say.

Lisa and her Dad did not feel close anymore, and this made her very unhappy. "I bet he's ashamed I'm his daughter," she thought.

*Favoritism and Stepsibs.* Parents and stepparents occasionally encourage competition among stepsibs in other ways. Stepparents bend over backward to welcome stepchildren into the new family, giving them kind words, praise, and gifts to make them feel welcome. Stepparents put their arms around stepchildren to make them feel loved and appreciated. Adults twist the rules for stepchildren and scold them less than they do their natural children.

As these stepparents try to win their stepchildren's approval and affection, their natural children are outraged at this two-faced behavior. They feel less important and less special to their natural parent than are their stepsibs. Natural children resent stepsibs receiving the parental affection that rightly belongs to them. They do not think it is fair for a parent to be strict with them while allowing their stepsibs to get away with murder.

When these things happen, natural children feel pushed aside, taken for granted, and unloved. As they see their stepsibs getting "goodies" they do not deserve, the competitive feelings among them grow stronger.

*Money and Stepsibs.* Money issues sometimes cause competition and jealousy among stepsibs. Stepfathers do not have a legal duty to spend money on their stepchildren, but most want to support their new family the best they can. Unfortunately, many stepfathers pay for two families and regularly send checks to their natural children living with the ex-wife. When these children visit their father, their stepsibs look to see how much money—in the form of new clothing, toys, and fun—their Dad spends on each set of children. If Dad buys his children clothes, bikes, or trips to play miniature golf, his stepchildren feel left out and jealous. If the visiting children see their stepsibs living in a beautiful home with their own rooms, plenty of games, and nice wardrobes, they feel left out and jealous.

To many, money seems like proof of love, and if young people do not receive a lot of material things from their parent or stepparent that their stepsibs do receive, they conclude that their Dad does not love them as much as his "other children."

*Visiting Stepsibs and Live-in Stepsibs.* Visiting stepsibs have other problems with each other. They resent new brothers and sisters living with their "real Dad" while they cannot. Visiting children do not like other children living in their old house, and they resent doing chores for a family with whom they do not really live. Visiting young people find it difficult to fit into the new family's routines or ways of doing things. More important, visiting stepsibs show competition and jealousy toward the live-in children because they feel unsure about how much their natural parent still loves them and how much he or she loves their stepsibs. Visiting stepsibs do not know where they stand, where they fit, and they seek to find out. They want to see whose side their natural parent takes when called upon to break up fights or settle arguments between the young people.

On the other side, the live-in children do not like having to share their room, take different seats at the table, or be forced to play with their visiting stepsibs. Live-in children do not like to see their parent and stepparent fuss over the visiting children, planning special treats or activities to make them feel welcome. All the attention shown visiting stepsibs makes live-in children feel left out and unimportant. Live-in children then feel rivalry with their visiting stepsibs for their parent's and stepparent's interest and attention. As difficult as it is for stepsibs to get along with each other, they are more likely to develop good relationships when all live together full time.

*How Stepsibs Relate to Each Other.* When stepsibs are jealous and competitive toward each other, they fight back. Some become closer to their stepparent, absent parent, at-home parent, or certain stepsibs in an effort to gain allies and support. Some form tight little groups and talk meanly about those family members left out. Others start mischief and hide stepsibs' shoes, throw stepsibs' clothing onto the greasy garage floor, or "accidentally" break their toys. Fights, teasing, and arguments become common in all types of families as rivalries surface, but arguments seem nastier in stepfamilies. Without a background of shared experiences and good will, stepsibs try in many hurtful ways to find where they fit and who loves whom the most.

At times, stepsibs get along very well. They all feel left out of the special bond their remarried parents share. They know the other children feel the same sadness, resentment, and loneliness that they feel, and the shared anger and hurt draws them together. They identify with one another and understand each other's problems. Occasionally, new stepsibs join forces to battle against their stepfamily. They all want to regain closeness with their natural parent, and many still dream about putting their first family back together. They may also unite to give one certain stepsib a rough time, making him or her the scapegoat for all their frustrations with their parent and with each other. Other stepsibs treat each other with friendliness and kindness because they like, admire, and respect their stepparent and want to extend this relationship to include the stepparent's children. In addition, when a remarriage appears solid and satisfying, and when a natural parent seems really happy in the new family, the children show more willingness to build good relationships with their stepsibs. The young people realize that this arrangement is going to be a long one, and they had better make the best of it.

*Fair and Equal Rules*

Blending two sets of young people with different rules, habits, and tastes into one family makes discipline tricky business. One child is used to strictly enforced rules about dress, talk, meals, homework, allowance, privileges, and responsibilities. The other is used to easygoing, relaxed rules. Stepfamilies must decide which rules to carry over, which to change, and what new rules to add.

Whoever has to adjust to new rules thinks it is unfair. If stepchildren have to start dressing formally for dinner, they say their parent favors the other children. If stepchildren see stepsibs inviting friends to stay the night, they say it is favoritism that prevents them from inviting their own friends to sleep over. If family members are supposed to take turns setting the table and washing the dishes, everyone watches closely to see who actually does those tasks. If "his" children have to do chores, "her" children also must do them. If "his" children stay up until 10 p.m. on school nights, "her" children expect to do likewise. If "his" children go to the movies, "her" children must go, too. All rules in a stepfamily must pass the fair-and-equal test.

In first families, parents make rules for young people on the basis of their age, sex, and maturity. They use common sense to decide that older children stay up later but take on more household responsibilities than younger children. Common sense tells parents that older children should finish their homework before watching TV or playing with friends. Common sense says that older children have greater personal expenses and need larger allowances than younger ones.

Stepfamilies see rules differently because both parents and children show tremendous sensitivity to "fair" and "equal." Stepfamilies feel the need to treat all children equally to show that they love all equally. Now, if "her" six-year-old daughter stays up until 10:30 p.m. on school nights while "his" twelve-year-old son goes to bed at 9:30, this decision shows favoritism. If "his" daughter clears the table after dinner, which takes ten minutes, while "her" son takes out the garbage, a job taking three minutes, this decision shows favoritism. If one stepsib must clean up her room today but the other is not told to do the same, this decision is also not fair or equal.

Rules in first families fit the individuals. Rules are appropriate but unequal. A teenager has more maturity, skills, and independence than a nine-year-old, and both deserve rules that fit and help each learn and grow. In stepfamilies, where all members watch closely to see where they fit and how much they are loved, unequal rules feel like unequal love, like unequal fairness. To try to treat all children in the family exactly alike creates ridiculous and truly unfair situations.

Stepparents cannot pretend that everyone in the family has the same relationship, and they need to set and enforce rules fairly. Favoritism may be real or imagined, but it is an important issue when stepsibs live together. Rules should fit the children's ages, merits, and maturity and should be kept by all children to whom they apply. When stepsibs challenge parents with cries of unfairness and favoritism, they really ask if they belong, if they are loved and valued. Stepparents and natural parents need to reassure them in more meaningful ways than taking away the rules. Anything else is truly unjust.

## A New Child in the Family

Remarried couples bring their own children from a first family to their marriage. These stepsibs have no blood ties and no shared histories. At first, only their parents' wedding and household unite them. They build their relationships starting as strangers.

Remarried couples sometimes want to have children of their own, for a variety of reasons. Feeling happy and confident in their marriage, they want to celebrate its permanence with a child whom both can love and raise together. Some remarried couples want to prove to themselves and to others their "success" at making a good marriage, and a baby becomes living proof. To others, having a child makes the new marriage "divorce-proof" because they believe they will work harder to solve their problems with the child as an extra reason to stay together. A few remarried couples believe having a baby will make them a "real" family, enabling them to erase their past mistakes by making their second family better than the first.

The reasons remarried couples have babies affect the ways family members relate to one another. Having children out of genuine love and commitment makes all stepfamily members feel the security and desire to work together. Having a child for any other reason does not increase feelings of security or build personal bonds for long.

When a stepfamily has new children, everyone else in the family becomes truly related by blood and history for the first time. The baby belongs to the whole family more than any of the individual members. The baby unites both sets of stepsibs as nothing before could. All the children adore the baby and want to take care of it. The baby is really "their" brother or sister.

What is more, the new baby signals the stability and permanence of the stepfamily. Parents and children feel secure in the relationship and expect their new family to last. This confidence and security encourage everyone to build better relationships with one another and to make their family solid.

Not all remarried couples, however, want new babies. Parents who already have children may not want to start over again with infants and their needs. Many stepparents believe their family has enough children already and do not have the money, time, energy, or interest to have more. Many stepparents are not young enough to have more children, or they may have careers they do not wish to give up.

Other stepparents do not want to have their own children because they are already working hard to make their stepfamily succeed, and they find it rough going. A stepfamily brings many problems to settle, and stepparents may not have the faith or confidence in their new marriage or family situation to risk having babies. In fact, when both partners have children from their first marriages, they are less likely to have children together. When young parents remarry or when one partner does not already have children, the possibility of having babies becomes greater.

*Problems With New Children in Stepfamilies.* Having a baby, however, does not always change stepfamily relationships for the better. The baby ends once and for all the stepchildren's fantasies of reuniting their divorced parents. To some, a new baby represents their parent's unfaithfulness to the first family; it seems as if the parent wants to stop caring about them and to love the baby instead. Older half brothers and half sisters feel left out. They resent losing their natural parent's attention and affection once again. This is especially true for visiting children, who cannot enjoy watching their half sib grow every day and who only feel less important to their natural parent when they visit.

Many older stepsibs have to baby-sit or play with the new child when they would rather be enjoying their own friends. Some older children look at the baby and feel left out because it really belongs to the new family while they do not. The baby has two real parents living together, but the older stepchildren do not, and they feel less important and less secure. The older children also resent having their half brother or half sister entitled to their parent's money, insurance, or inheritance and view the baby as a little thief.

At times, older half sisters feel competitive with their mother or stepmother and want to have their own boyfriend to prove they, too, can be attractive and desirable to men. In their minds, these older half sisters feel so left out of their parent's love when the baby arrives that they imagine how nice it would be to have their own baby to love, who would love them back, and to whom they would really belong.

Babies in stepfamilies bring mixed blessings. Many times they unite already happy stepfamilies and bring all members together as nothing else could. Sometimes the situation does not work that way.

Babies by themselves do little to help stepfamilies feel whole and united. The love, attention, fairness, and patience shown stepchildren as well as the genuine commitment and love shared by the married couple make stepfamilies work. When young people feel sure of their parent's continued love, affection, and interest, and when they can accept the new marriage, they will also be able to accept their new half brothers and half sisters.

*The Question of Names*

Stepfamilies try to feel like whole families despite the many differences they bring. When children are "Sally and Mark Jones" while their mother is "Mrs. John O'Donnell" or when stepbrothers and stepsisters are "Klines" and "Smiths," everyone remembers that they do not really belong together. When stepchildren call their stepdad "Joe," while their stepbrothers and sisters call him "Daddy," everyone feels like part of an ill-fitting jigsaw.

All the complicated feelings stepparents and stepchildren have for each other come out when they have to introduce each other or describe their relationship to outsiders. Are these "my wife's children," "our children," or simply "Sally, Mark, and Eric?" Names reflect the confusion stepfamily members feel about who they are and where they belong.

Names define relationships with others. The term "step-" makes people feel awkward and ashamed, as if they were not good enough to be the real thing. "Step-" originally meant that one parent had died and the survivor had remarried. It also suggests one step away from the real thing, a degree less love and commitment between adults and children.

Inside the new family, members decide what to call each other. Stepchildren must quickly decide what to call their stepparent. Not only is this a practical matter, but the name chosen will also reflect the young people's answer to "What does this person mean to me?"

Most stepchildren prefer to call stepparents by their first name, by a special nickname, or by a version of Mom or Dad different from what they call their natural parent. Young people view relationships with stepparents as separate from their relationship with their natural parents, and they want to respect that difference. Preferring to call stepparents by their first name or a nickname implies no criticism. It simply means a comfortable place from which they can develop ties with their stepparents while respecting the bonds they have with their natural parents.

Stepparents sometimes dislike this solution. They want a title like "Mother" or "Father" to show more control over the young people, to prove they are as good as "real" parents, or to prove they have won the young people's acceptance of their marriage. These stepparents insist that their stepchildren call them "Mother" or "Father" in an attempt to gain respect, obedience, and love from the young people.

In doing this, they force the young people to lie. Calling people "Mom" or "Dad" does not automatically create a relationship.

Only time together sharing interests and affection and building trust can do that.

Deciding on a name for his stepfather was not easy for Glenn, age eleven. Riding his new ten-speed bike, he muttered to himself. It was a great bike, and Glenn was proud of it, but he thought it had cost him too much.

His mother had remarried a few months ago, and while Glenn did not like the whole idea of her being married to someone other than his Dad, he tried to make the best of it. Frank, his stepdad, was okay, but Glenn resented his trying to be the big man at home. Frank's kids visited them on weekends, but Frank wanted to be called "Dad" every day. He had asked Glenn to call him "Dad," but Glenn said no, he already had one Dad. Glenn wanted to call him "Frank," but his stepdad thought that did not show enough respect.

Since the two could not agree on a name, they barely spoke for two tense months. Glenn's Mom asked him to call Frank "Dad," but he could not do that, even for her; the word stuck in his throat. Glenn offered to call him "Pop," and while Frank was not thrilled with that name, he agreed. Glenn felt as if he were giving away a special private part of himself whenever he called Frank "Pop," but he continued anyway. Three weeks later the ten-speed arrived, a gift from Frank. Glenn felt as if he had been "bought."

Names for parents and stepparents also create tension among stepsibs. Natural children call their mother "Mom" and their father "Dad." To hear strange kids, their stepsibs, using those special names makes the natural children jealous. They tell themselves, This is our real father or mother. These other children have no right to call them "Mom" or "Dad." Mom and Dad love us because we are their real children, and we want to keep their love and affection for ourselves. If our stepsibs call them "Mom" or "Dad," maybe our folks will start loving them as much as they love us. Maybe more. That would be awful!

On the other hand, children who call a stepparent by his/her first name, a nickname, or variations of Mom or Dad still feel second-best whenever they hear their stepsibs calling that same adult "Mom" or "Dad." Because they are not this adult's natural children, they feel they have less influence, are less valued, and receive less love than do the natural children.

Last names also create problems for stepfamily members. Last names tell the world who we are and who our father is. Many children feel close and loving ties with their natural father and want to keep his last name. Their natural father plays a large part in their life and feelings, and keeping their family name keeps those ties strong. It helps them feel loyal and shows their love for their absent father even as they live happily in a stepfamily.

When mothers and children have different last names, it publicly announces that the mother has had another husband. Last names have practical and emotional meanings that must be understood and accepted.

Merry, age ten, wanted the best of both worlds. She wanted to be a Tanner like her Dad and also to be a Taylor like her Mom and stepdad. Merry loved all the adults in her live and wanted to belong to everyone. She felt awkward whenever she introduced her mother to friends or teachers because they had different last names. It made her feel different and weird.

Merry doodled both names in her notebook. "Merry Tanner" "Merry Taylor," "Merry T." At least both names began with the same letter.

One day, her stepfamily visited the seashore and spent two nights in a motel. Merry asked her folks if she could sign the guest book herself. She took the pen from the counter and wrote, "Merry Taylor" on the register beneath her mother's and stepdad's name. Now she felt as if she really belonged.

Differing last names occasionally confuse outsiders as well. Older children wonder how their friends will find their phone number if the book lists only their stepparent's last name. Schools, Boy Scouts, and other organizations do not know which set of parents to invite to special events. Should the custodial parent and spouse alone receive the invitations on graduation, inductions, and award ceremonies? Few organizations even ask for names and addresses of absent parents for official records, assuming the custodial parents will handle the personal details or that the absent parent is not interested.

Some stepfamilies think they solve the name problem by allowing children to call themselves by their stepfather's name. Stepchildren introduce themselves, sign hotel registers, enter school records or social security cards using that name just to pretend theirs is a first family. Parents are embarrassed to admit a previously failed marriage and believe that looking like a "real" family makes it so. Not only do these families create legal problems for themselves and their children later on, but they prevent themselves and their children from accepting the reality of their situation. Names are identity. People need to accept themselves as individuals if they are to be happy with themselves. Pretending children have other last names keeps stepfamily members from accepting the family and allowing their relationships to grow naturally.

When stepfamily members become comfortable with their past and accept their new arrangement as real and satisfying in its own right, they know they have nothing to hide and nothing for which to apologize. At that point, two last names in one stepfamily pose no problems.

*The Question of Adoption.* Stepchildren sometimes think adoption would make them feel that they truly belonged in their stepfamily. Adoption would legally give them the same last name as their natural parent and stepparent. Adoption permits stepparents to sign medical release and driver's license forms and allows children to inherit money and property from them. It makes the relationship permanent and gives them the same legal status as any children born of the marriage. If the remarried parent later divorces or dies, the young people still legally belong with their stepparent. With adoption, many youngsters finally know how and where they fit into their new family.

On the other hand, many stepchildren want to keep their emotional and legal ties with their natural father. Even if they cannot live together all the time, at least their last name stays the same. These young people deeply love their natural father and are glad to have this clear link to him. The fact that they have a different last name from their mother, stepfather, or stepsibs does not bother them at all. They are proud to keep their own last name, which tells them who they are and where they belong.

Adoption has its good points and its bad points. While it gives stepchildren legal standing and gives all stepfamily members the same last name, it does not automatically bring closeness, trust, or love into the relationship. The emotional ties between individuals give their relationship its meaning and pleasure. Name changes and legal papers do not. Furthermore, breaking all ties with natural parents is difficult. Adoption breaks the last legal links children have to their first family. Adoption is not merely a practical matter; it is a very emotional one as well, affecting the way individuals see and value themselves.

In adoption, the natural parent must sign legal papers giving up rights and ties to the children. In some states parental consent to adoption is not necessary if the parent was not given legal custody as part of the divorce settlement. When the legal parent cannot be found, the court may decide that parental rights have been given up by neglect and grant adoption without the absent parent's signature.

Sometimes, the children themselves ask the stepparent to adopt them. Older children who have lived with a stepparent for years and have grown to love him or her deeply, ask to be adopted. These young people want to make their relationship "official." The stepparent seems like a "real" parent, and the young people want to tell themselves and everyone else that the bond is good and permanent. When the absent natural parent has died or is no longer actively involved with the children, many youngsters seek adoption by their stepparent.

Many reasons exist for natural parents' agreeing to their children's adoption by stepparents. Consent means giving up visiting rights and no longer having to pay child care. These natural parents, usually but not always fathers, may want to give up their children to stepparents. They never visit the children and have no strong loving relationship with them. They may want to forget their past mistakes by legally and emotionally letting go of the children. Other absent parents love their children in their own way but believe the young people would be happier if they belonged to their stepfamily. They consent to adoption in the children's "best interests." These are never easy decisions for natural parents to make.

Many reasons exist for refusing to allow adoption. For some natural parents, no matter how great the geographical or emotional distance between themselves and their children, they will never allow the stepparent to adopt them. These absent parents have excellent relationships with their children even at a distance and would never consider allowing them to be adopted. Other absent parents care about their children but don't want to work at keeping their relationship strong. Visiting, writing, or phoning become unpleasant chores, rarely done. Still other parents do not want their ex-spouse to receive one more thing from the divorce and so refuse to agree to adoption. They do not really care about the children; they just want to keep the legal tie. These parents want to spite their ex-spouse, not show love and commitment to their children. In all cases, the decision to permit adoption is not a simple one. Nevertheless, one third of all U.S. adoptions are of stepchildren.

Adoption is best in certain situations. When the young people have long and enduring bonds with their stepfather, ties based on shared trust, respect, and love, adoption gives legal permanence to their already solid relationship. When children are very young and have few if any bonds with their absent parent, adoption by the stepparent becomes possible. If children's natural father is deceased, or if their mother never married the father, adoption by the stepparent becomes a possible choice.

In some cases adoption is not a good choice. Those include situations in which the mother is still angry with her ex-husband and wants to hurt him by legally taking away his children through adoption by her new husband. Another situation in which adoption is inadvisable is when a remarried couple cannot have children of their own and see adoption of one partner's natural children as a way to end the other partner's childlessness. While adoption makes a stepparent a legal parent, only building strong and satisfying bonds with stepchildren can make a stepparent feel like a real parent. Adoption is not a substitute for building genuine relationships.

Similarly, some remarried parents believe that adoption of their children by their new spouse erases their past failures. Changing the young people's legal status and last name, however, does not help the parent or the community to forget the sad ending of the first marriage. Adoption does not magically change a stepfamily into a "real" family. Stepfamilies are already "real" families; they can never be "first" families. All the legal papers in the world cannot erase memories, cannot destroy emotional bonds between people, and cannot forgive people for their past errors. Legal papers cannot create emotional ties of trust, love, and loyalty. Only people can do that.

# CHAPTER VII

## Adolescents in Stepfamilies

Adolescence is the worst time to become a stepchild. Researchers agree on this point. Teens' goals of developing personal independence and a sense of themselves as unique and separate individuals conflict with their new stepfamily's wish to build a united family. Teens have strong ties with their natural parents and their first family. They seldom want to let a newcomer into their home. Teenagers do not want to learn new rules or obey new limits. They already disagree with most of the old rules and limits as they try to separate themselves from their family. They want to start thinking and acting for themselves as free agents, and they do this by testing and challenging family values and beliefs. Teens face losses that they feel deeply and that make them distrust relationships with others. They also begin behaving as aware sexual individuals trying gradually to understand and accept themselves in new and sometimes upsetting ways.

Adolescence, the years between eleven and twenty-one, brings stress to all families, first families included. Linked with all the extra problems of stepfamilies, teens and their new families find themselves under additional stress.

### What Teens Bring to Stepfamilies

*Trying to Separate from the Family.* Teenagers have strong feelings about divorce. They are angry with their parents for divorcing. They feel sad, empty, or betrayed by their absent parent, even if they had argued frequently with that parent before the separation. Teens worry about their parents' moods and health, and they wonder how the adults will manage to care for the family. Who will pay the grocery, heat, telephone bills? Who will pay the rent? Will they be able to afford new clothes? Can they still plan to attend college or professional school?

Young people are frightened of a world so complex and unpredictable. Their sense of safety and rightness seems ripped away. If they cannot count on their parents' love for each other, they cannot depend on their parents' love for them, either. If teens cannot depend on the most important and basic things in their lives, what can they count on?

Just as adolescents start to move out of the family and deal more and more with people and events on their own, divorce or death shakes their confidence in the world as a manageable place. At a time when they need all the family support and self-confidence they can muster to begin acting as mature and independent people, the important props crash down around them.

Teens are individuals and respond to this situation according to their own personality, needs, abilities, and past experience. For many, divorce and death naturally mean sadness about the loss. The young people first grieve, then go on with their life. Frequently teens have already begun separating from their family. They view their parents as real persons with good and bad points. Parents no longer seem all-knowing or all-powerful; they are simply people with their own abilities, interests, needs, and limitations. When teens' parents divorce, the young people see the separation and anger as the parents' problems, not theirs. They do not blame themselves or hold anger toward their parents longer than necessary. Anger costs energy, and these young people prefer to spend their energies on more satisfying activities.

These young people understand the realities. They know about money and are aware of their family's financial status. They know whether there is enough money this year for their new winter coat, and they understand if they cannot have a new stereo as their friends do. Teens accept having to move into a smaller home or having to share a room with stepsibs. They may not like the situation and they may wish it were different, but teens accept what is and go on.

Adolescents have their own lives. They have their own friends, schools, sports, hobbies, plans, and dreams apart from their family. While their home life changes, other special and personal parts of their life remain the same. These teens take on extra chores at home. Added responsibilities mean gaining more skills, more information, and more confidence. Even when they become a stepfamily member, they cooperate at home. They still think and plan ahead for their separate future. They realize that their home is a place to live for a while, but their plans and dreams remain their own.

Divorce and death do not affect all teens this way. For teens who have not yet separated themselves emotionally from their parents, their own life seems completely overturned by the sad event. They are very angry at their parents for "ruining" their life and for stealing their trust and their dreams. Young people feel betrayed and view their parents' problems as theirs, too. They want to take sides and see one parent as totally at fault and the other parent as all good and a tragic victim. These teens refuse to depend on any relationship again because they do not want to risk the tremendous letdown if the relationship ends. They think marriage is a roulette game in which people use tricks to get what they want. All is luck or deceit.

As a result of these ideas and feelings about loss and relationships, some teens protect themselves from other ties. They become very possessive of their "good" parent and "good" brothers and sisters as if to guarantee that those relationships will last. They are extremely jealous when an outsider such as a stepparent enters their family to steal the affections of their remaining parent.

Other teens who distrust relationships promise themselves they will never again become that close or dependent on anyone else. They distance themselves from those persons who love them. These teens refuse to go along with household rules and limits; they bitterly argue and fight with parents and stepparents, brothers, sisters, and stepsibs. They say they do not give two cents for anyone in the world. They cut themselves off from others by their anger and nastiness to protect themselves from the pain and hurt of loss.

Teenagers who have not separated emotionally from their family sometimes act as if they were already independent before they have acquired the necessary skills or confidence to act as mature, responsible individuals. They turn to friends, cars, drugs, alcohol, sex, and adventure as ways to feel good about themselves and to prove that they do not need their family. They have their own lives and will make their own choices. At least they can decide what to do. They have the control and the power to say "Yes" or "No." Having good times without giving thought to responsibilities or to the future lets these teens feel less helpless, less afraid. The choices they make may not be in their best interests, but at least they are their own choices. Doing what they want makes them feel in charge of their own lives again.

These young people feel powerless in a frightening world. They seek to control whatever they can. These teens cannot undo the divorce and cannot undo their stepfamily. They cannot concentrate on their studies for thinking about their unhappiness and the unfairness of the situation. Now they find things they can control. With friends, alcohol, drugs, or sex, they can make their own choices. They can feel good about themselves for a few hours and feel in control of their lives as they cannot at home. They can have angry outbursts at home and influence their family's moods. They can upset their parent and stepparent by disobeying rules and by rejecting the stepparent's offers of friendship. At a time when young people are supposed to be "in charge" and "in control," these teens appear to be independent, free agents who do not need or want help or advice from anyone. The truth, however, may be quite different, and they remain unhappy and immature.

In other homes, divorce and remarriage keep teens immature in different ways. Some teens feel so frightened and upset by the drastic changes that they are afraid to start separating emotionally or physically from their family. Everything seems so complicated or so hard. These teens fear making mistakes or suffering the pains and disappointments that come with growing up and acting on their own. They prefer playing with younger children, who make fewer demands on them than do their peers. They would rather baby-sit than go to the school dance. They would rather stay home and clean house or fix meals so their single parent will not be lonely. They worry for weeks about what topic to use for an English term paper, sit for hours trying to decide what outfit to wear the next day. They spend weeks trying to figure out which boy to allow to escort them to the prom and finally decide not to go at all rather than choose the "wrong" date.

These young people tear themselves apart trying to make even the simplest decisions because they lack confidence in their judgment. Although many of them seem to be helpful and responsible sons and daughters, their reasons for avoiding independence keep them immature longer than they need to be.

Occasionally, teens become overly close to their single parent during the time before remarriage. They become their parent's companion and best friend, exchanging their most private thoughts and feelings. They sit in "Mother's seat" or "Father's seat" at dinner, act as hostess or host for their single parent's parties, or serve as companion for their single parent at social engagements. These teens feel important and valued as never before, and that makes them feel good about themselves. At the same time, they see less need to make friends their own age or engage in teenage activities. Basketball games or window shopping in the mall seem juvenile and silly compared with the special life they have with their single parent.

When their single parent remarries, not only do these teens lose their special role at home but they also lack outside friends with whom to spend time and have fun. Then these immature teens even more strongly resent their stepparent for taking over their place at home because it feels as if they have nothing meaningful left.

*Trying to Build an Identity.* Teens work to define themselves. They want to know what they are about, what makes them unique. They want to know their abilities and their limits. They want to understand what makes them excited and happy and what turns them off. Teens learn these things by watching how their parents behave as adults. Are they patient and fair, or are they more concerned with their own lives? Do they set rules for their own convenience or to help the young people learn to make better decisions? How do men in this society act? How do women act? Watching their parents provides young people with major lessons in how adults are supposed to act and how the teens as men and women themselves are supposed to act. Parents serve as models by which teens measure themselves and learn proper ways of behaving.

Young people also learn about themselves by observing how their parents treat them and how their friends and teachers treat them. If others relate to them as friendly, intelligent, and sensitive persons, the teens perceive themselves as friendly, intelligent, and sensitive. If others tell teens they are talented in math or sports or mechanics, the young people believe they have talents in those areas. Teens learn to see themselves as others see them and by their own perception of success and failure.

Young people also learn about themselves through their activities and experiences. When classmates regularly tell them their troubles and ask for advice, the teens feel like loyal friends and good listeners. The more they listen to friends, the more understanding and the sounder their advice becomes. When teens are able to fix a broken lamp and start dinner on their own, they feel confident about their skills and develop more abilities. When teens are able to think about what they want, consider different paths to achieve their goal, select a plan and try it out, and then reach their goal, they build confidence in their ability to make successful decisions.

When teens ride in cars with friends who drive too fast, or have their favorite teachers look at them with disappointment for skipping classes, they learn what they do not like about themselves. When teens feel bad about their actions and take time to think about why, they also learn about themselves: They learn how to make a more satisfying decision the next time.

Divorce and death complicate teens' search for themselves. One parent lives elsewhere or is no longer alive. That model for adult behavior is no longer available to watch every day. Some teens wonder how they are supposed to learn to act as mature adults when only one parent remains to teach them.

Teenage boys living with their mother show special concern about this issue. Without Dad at home, some teenage boys question how tough they are supposed to act. When are they supposed to show tenderness and support for others? What values and ideals should they hold? Watching Dad taught them so much without his having to say a word.

Much of what these boys saw their Dad do, they liked. Some of what they saw, they did not like. But they loved and respected their father. They felt loyalty to him because they had so much in common. They were both men and related to the larger world through that perspective.

Even when young men have a stepfather, uncles, and older male friends at hand, they feel they most resemble their natural father and need his personal guidance. Many times, these young men have ties to their father and visit him often, but the relationship may be only skin-deep. Not sharing their daily lives, neither father nor son wants to risk their relationship by becoming too serious and possibly exposing hurt or angry feelings that might separate them further.

When teenage boys feel confused about how to behave as men, they often imagine how their father would act and use that imaginary model for their own actions. Occasionally, they overdo what they think their Dad would want in an attempt to find the "right" way to act. They try to act as they imagine their father would act to show their continued loyalty and love for him.

Occasionally, teenage boys who have lived with their mother for years suddenly ask to live with their father in order to have him available as a model. That does not mean they no longer love their mother. Rather, they believe that at this point in their life they need their father's guidance more.

Teenage girls also need their father in order to learn about themselves as females. Watching Dad deal with Mom shows girls one way in which men behave with women and how some women respond. Having a father at home giving them attention, complimenting them on their new dresses or hairstyles, giving them hugs and kisses lets girls know what it is like to relate to men. Caring, attentive fathers let girls feel good about themselves as females. If they can make Dad happy and pleased, girls gain confidence in their ability to please other men, too. In divorced families, teenage girls also lack important adult models.

The same modeling situation holds true for teenagers and their mother. Needing attention and approval from parents of both sexes, teens sharply feel their absence. They need the approval of their opposite parent to help them learn how to act with others of that sex. When these parents remarry, the new spouse gets much of the natural parent's attention and affection while the adults work to build a strong marriage. Less time for teens means less reassurance for them as young men and women. Teens resent their stepparent's replacing them with their natural parent, especially during these years when they are learning so much about themselves, as well as after for so long having the parent all to themselves.

Bitter rivalries between teens and their stepparent of the same sex sometimes result. Teenage girls compete with their stepmother for their father's continued interest, and teenage boys vigorously challenge their stepfather for their mother's attention. Teens start arguments with the stepparent or try to start arguments between the couple. Sometimes they begin flirting with their natural parent, trying to gain their parent's attention and interest the way they see the stepparent doing. Boys bring their mother flowers and girls greet their father at the door with the newspaper and a cocktail. Teens show high awareness of their same-sex stepparent's dress and attitudes, noticing every new outfit and every behavior. Teens wonder if they are as good-looking, as desirable, or as important to their opposite-sex parent as the new spouse is.

Beth, age fourteen, wondered whether she were still special to her Dad since his remarriage. She moved her chair closer to his so she could look over his shoulder at the newspaper. She beat her stepmother downstairs and fixed Dad's coffee. She even made blueberry muffins the way he liked them.

That was the way it used to be before Dad remarried. It was quiet and peaceful, and they were alone together. Beth was glad her stepmother liked to sleep late. Promptly each morning, Beth put Dad's briefcase near the door and took his jacket from the closet. Dad hugged and kissed her and whispered, "Have a great day, sweetheart." Their morning routine felt just as it used to. Beth smiled as she cleaned the kitchen and got ready for school. Dad was still her fellow and no one could ever change that.

When teens cannot gain their opposite-sex parent's attention and reassurance about themselves as young men and women, they sometimes look to build their self-confidence as sexual persons through outside relationships. They begin dating and having steady boyfriends or girlfriends who let them feel attractive, important, and desirable. Some become sexually active before they are really ready in order to gain approval as a valuable and desirable person. Sexual intimacy lets them feel good about themselves as men and women, for a short time at least.

Fortunately, teens have many fine models of adult male and female behavior. They may have ongoing ties with their absent parent and can watch the adult's behavior as well as feel the adult's pride in the teen's own maleness or femaleness. Many teens have a loving stepparent who provides a good model and shows real interest and affection. Relatives, teachers, counselors, and friends all help in these ways, too.

In addition, older teens have more confidence in their own sexuality. They have felt their parents' continued support and have their own experiences with boyfriends and girlfriends to make them feel good about their attractiveness and ability to build satisfying boy-girl relationships. These teens also understand their parent's need for physical and emotional intimacy and are glad that the companionship with the stepparent makes both adults happy persons and more loving parents. These older teens know and like themselves, so they have nothing to prove. They do not need extra reassurance about where they stand as men and women because they already know they have what it takes to build deeply meaningful relationships in every way.

What is more, as teens mature, they gain confidence in their own opinions and decisions. They do not need their parents' advice or approval for every action because they have time and again acted responsibly and successfully on their own. With experience teens have built the skills and gained the information needed to act independently and effectively.

When this happens, teens look more realistically at their parents. They see the adults' faults and weaknesses, but they do not blame their parents for past mistakes. Mature teens see their parents as people who are human and who sometimes make bad choices. They hear their parents say hurtful, unfair, or ignorant things. They watch their parents make the same errors over and over again. Teens see their parents as unhappy, disappointed persons who simply cannot do any better.

The faults belong to the parents, not to the teens. Mature teens do not have to be unhappy, angry, abusive, or uncaring because of how their parents act. Teens do not have to fail at jobs or at relationships because their parents have failed. They do not have to set lower goals or have fewer dreams because their parents cannot achieve what they want. Mature teens feel separate from their parents and can make their own choices about how to live their lives. They stop feeling deprived or angry with their parents for disappointing them: Parents are the way they are, and nothing will change that. For the first time understanding and accepting their parents allows teens to feel truly free to understand and accept themselves.

When they separate themselves from their parents, many teens decide that they love their parents but do not want to be like them.

Mature teens and their parents see the world differently. They have different values, different beliefs, different ways of solving problems. Mature teens no longer need their parents as role models. They feel free to choose their own models by which to guide their thoughts and actions. They feel free to admire stepparents, neighbors, teachers, or friends who live their lives in ways the young people respect. Mature, confident, self-aware young people select their own models and find the support they need to grow into true maturity.

## Teens' Feelings About Stepfamilies

*Feelings About Independence.* At this time in their lives, teens try to move out of their family circle and test their own decisions and actions in the larger world. Teens want to understand themselves better so they can make choices for today and tomorrow that truly suit them. Unfortunately, adolescents' needs sometimes conflict with their stepfamily's needs.

For one thing, stepfamilies often ask teens to change roles. Teens can no longer remain the man or woman of their home. They can no longer be their parent's best friend, confidant, or sole companion. They can no longer "parent" their younger brothers and sisters. Teens lose the special place they held in a single-parent family when a stepparent arrives.

Although that position was sometimes difficult and time-consuming, it allowed the young people to feel needed, important, and good about their ability to keep their parent and their family happy. Teens valued the special bond with their single parent and now resent the stepparent's pushing them aside. Although many teens are secretly glad to have less work to do at home, they also feel angry, used, and useless. Through remarriage, teens lose their important place in their family and wonder if they have also lost their parent's love.

For another thing, teens work to build their own life and learn new ways of thinking and acting. When home life stays the same, teens feel free to spend energies working toward their own independence. They can take risks and test new behavior outside the home because they can always return to its safety to regroup, plan, and start out again.

Stepfamilies, however, bring new rules and new routines. Meals are served at different hours. Food tastes and looks different. Stepbrothers and stepsisters must share bedrooms. New chores are assigned. Teens may have to speak differently, dress differently, or roll up the toothpaste tube differently to please their new stepparent.

Furthermore, teens want to spend more time with friends and activities away from home. Their personal life apart from their family becomes very important. Relationships with friends teach teens how to act successfully in the larger world. At the same time, stepfamilies want to build togetherness to feel like a "real" family. Stepparents expect all children, teens included, to join family activities. As teenagers want more freedom to be away from home, stepfamilies insist they remain in the home. This sets the scene for many arguments.

*Feelins About New Roles and Routines.* Teens did not ask for all these changes. The old ways worked fine for them. They already have their habits, personalities, and ways of doing things. This is true of teens in all families: first families, single-parent families, and stepfamilies. Teens see no reason to change something that works.

In the meantime, stepparents want to feel active and important in their new family by setting new rules and limits. They want to take charge, prove themselves an able parent, and make their family "shape up" or simply function better. Parents wanting to please their new mate go along with these changes and expect the teens to go along, too. Stepparents with little experience with teens sometimes expect instant agreement or cooperation and become all the more frustrated when the teens argue and act rudely. With the reality so different from the expectation, extra conflict follows.

Even teens in a first family argue about rules and limits. To young people testing their ability to reason and form their own opinions, family rules look ridiculous or unfair. What law says bedtime has to be 9:30 p.m.? What law says curfew should be 8 p.m. on school nights and 11 p.m. on weekends? Where is it written that teens have to visit relatives at Christmas when they would rather go to a friend's party? Politics, religion, morality, and taste all become open targets for argument as teens test their parents' ideas to see which make sense and which do not. Verbal pushing and pulling are natural parts of teens' households. Enter stepparents with their own interests, habits, and rules and teens find even more to attack. The many natural feelings teens have about themselves and their family grow one hundred times larger when added to the extra resentments they already feel about their stepfamily.

*Feelings About Discipline.* Changes at home frequently involve discipline. A stepparent not only wants to set new rules and limits but also wants teens to meet them. Teens challenge family limits anyway, but they deeply resent this stranger's trying to act like a parent and telling them what to do. When a stepparent begins acting like a parent, therefore, teens fight twice as hard: They fight the rules and they fight the stepparent's enforcing of the rules.

As discussed in Chapter VI, discipline is a confusing issue in stepfamilies. Many stepparents want the obedience and respect due a natural parent and try to control stepchildren as a way to take a rightful place in the stepfamily. Other stepparents believe rule setting and enforcing belongs to the natural parent, and they back away from involvement with discipline. Many natural parents themselves feel uncertain about how much they want their new mate to set limits and keep the young people in line.

Teens quickly see the adults' confusion about who has the last word in the stepfamily and use the confusion to do what they want. They sometimes start the adults arguing with each other. Unless both adults agree about discipline in the stepfamily, everyone grows more tense and angry.

With teens, setting and keeping limits means arguments under the best conditions. In a stepfamily, the natural parent should be the adult directly involved with the young people's behavior. All young people need clear and reasonable limits. Teens have the maturity to sit down with parent and stepparent and together spell out rules that all consider fair and proper for growing persons with certain skills and abilities. Teens should have a say in the rules by which they live. They have valid opinions about dating, curfews, homework, part-time jobs, and household chores that deserve a hearing.

Parents, however, have the legal and moral responsibility to guide and protect their children. They must have the last word. Effective parents give teens the freedom to grow and act within the limits set by the teens' abilities, maturity, and proven responsibility. As teens do more on their own successfully, as they make good decisions about how to act, parents allow more room for them to make decisions.

Stepparents help most in this area when they encourage the young people to speak their minds about rules and limits, to make suggestions about rules that seem fair and appropriate. Wise stepparents understand that teens need less "parenting" than do their younger brothers and sisters. They help teens when they encourage their spouse to listen to the teens' ideas about rules affecting them. If teens can complete their homework, earn good grades, and still talk with friends for thirty minutes each night, let them. If teens drive safely to school for play rehearsals, pay for their own gas or barter for gas by doing chores at home, and keep their grades high, let them.

When teens have a say in making the rules, they are more willing to keep them. Teens need different limits than their younger siblings because they have more skills and better judgment. If they do not, teens need supervised chances to develop them.

Stepparents also help teens with discipline when they permit the natural parent to be the active rule enforcer. Teens resist rules, but they love and respect their natural parent. They want the parent to be proud of their growing ability to make good choices. The stepparent is still a stranger for whom the teens feel no trust or respect. Stepparent and teens need time and chances to learn more about each other, to gain understanding and appreciation of each other, before the teens want to listen to and obey the stepparent. Until that time, the natural parent needs to set and enforce the limits.

Sometimes, however, stepparents and teens never build strong bonds of respect and appreciation. The teens listen only to their natural parent, and that is the way it is. Stepparents who resent their stepchildren's loyalty to their natural parent and who charge into the stepfamily with strong arms and a loud voice determined to take control of wayward teens find only anger, rebellion, and constant battles. Stepparents may force stepchildren to obey for the moment, but they cannot force respect or willing cooperation. Unless stepparents want to become twenty-four-hour police, they cannot force stepchildren to obey when the young people are out of sight.

Teens do not need an additional parent. They need a wise and caring adult friend whose opinions they respect. They need love and affection and respect. Stepparents do well to choose this model for their relationship with teenagers if they want to have an important and influential role in the young people's lives.

*Feelings About Belonging to Two Families.* Teens in stepfamilies belong to two families, one at home and one with their absent parent. Teens love and feel loyalty to both natural parents and wonder whether that loyalty will permit them to like, admire, or love their stepparent. When teens and older children begin to see their stepparent as kind, thoughtful, and enjoyable, they sometimes feel as if caring for the stepparent makes them traitors to their absent parent.

Teens struggle with themselves to hold back any fondness or appreciation for their stepparent because they fear losing their absent parent's love. They do not understand that they can love their natural parent as well as their stepparent without taking anything special from either one. When an absent parent demands teens' loyalty by expecting them to dislike their stepparent, the parent shows great unfairness to the teenagers. Loving parents want their children to have satisfying relationships with others, knowing that the more love and support they receive, the happier they will be and the more confidently they will mature.

When a stepparent tries to be a replacement parent, expecting instant love, instant obedience, or instant respect from stepchildren, the young people become angry and resentful that this stranger would dare try to take their natural parent's place. When a stepparent tells teens to put away pictures or gifts from their absent parent, teens become furious. Photos of their first family, scrapbooks, albums, or old cufflinks tell teens about themselves, about who they are. Their absent parent and their experiences together remain important parts of their personality. Remembrances from an absent parent tell teens that both parents loved and valued them. Young people need these mementos even though they feel sad-happy when they look at them. Asking young people to deny their past tells them to deny important parts of themselves, and it only further strains relations between teens and their stepparent.

Teens' growing confidence and independence allows them to need fewer visits with their absent parent in order to keep their strong ties. They know each other very well and feel sure of each other's interest and love. Teens also have their own friends and interests that play increasingly important parts in their lives.

At times, young people think their absent parent's need to visit with them is greater than their need to visit with the parent. They feel an obligation to visit the absent parent when what they would rather do is help their friends fix the used car they recently bought or sit with friends and listen to music. Duty and loyalty are important to teens, and they do not want to disappoint their absent parent by being selfish and staying away.

This is a time when all parents and young people should talk openly about their relationship and decide how to change their visiting schedule to permit the young people more choices. Loving parents are proud as their teens take steps toward mature friendships and independence, and they do not feel let down when the teens sometimes prefer to spend time with friends. Rather than meaning that the parent-teen relationship is less important, it means the two have enough trust and confidence that they no longer need to see one another so often to keep the ties strong and satisfying to both.

An issue many a stepfamily faces in this regard is the effort of the absent parent to make the children "comfortable" when they visit. Young people often resent the inclusion of stepcousins, stepgrandparents, or other outsiders on visits the children believe should be *their* time with the absent parent. The natural parent and stepparent need to remind the young people of the absent parent's well-meaning intention to give them an interesting time during the visit, especially by including children their own age to play with. The natural parent needs to be sensitive to the children's wish for special time alone with their absent parent, as well as to his or her perception of their needs for playmates, entertainment, and acceptance of their larger family.

Now and then, teens see their absent parent's home as an escape from problems. Teens have arguments with natural parent and stepparent, stepbrothers and stepsisters about everything from hair in the bathroom sink to having friends visit after school. Teens do not like losing their special place in the family, they do not like the new routines and rules. They do not like having a stepparent tell them what to do. The meaner the stepparent, the nicer the absent parent seems. The more demanding the stepparent, the more generous and loving the absent parent appears. The absent parent may have said, "If you are unhappy at home, give me a call and pack your bags.

You can always live with me." Teens tell themselves they have somewhere else to live if things become too tense at home. Sometimes absent parents welcome their teenagers into their home for a few days or weeks. They want to help and feel secretly glad the young people prefer them to their other parent and the stepparent. Usually the teens soon find that living with their absent parent is not as they imagined. This parent also has rules and limits. He or she may have remarried, and the teens now have another stepparent or stepsibs with whom to deal. With daily living, the absent parent seems less kind, less flexible, less generous than remembered. The young people have simply traded one set of problems for another. Given a chance for all involved to cool off and think about how their own attitudes and actions made the home situation worse than it had to be, many teens and parents want a face-saving way to return to their regular family.

Randy, age sixteen, could have used a face-saving answer. He felt as though he had been walking along this road for hours, thinking. He had lived with his natural father and stepmother for the past six weeks, but things were not working out well. Dad worked night shifts at the plant, and Randy rarely saw him. His stepmother treated him as if he were a nuisance, just more laundry and more dishes to wash.

Randy wanted to return to his mother and stepfather, but he thought he had lost that opportunity. His mom and stepdad had gone out for the evening and told him not to have company while they were gone. He was supposed to finish his homework and babysit for his half sister. Randy reasoned that if the movie his folks were seeing ended at 10:30 p.m., there was time for his friend to come over and leave by 10:15. His folks would never know the difference.

Who asked his folks to choose a different movie and return home early? Randy stood frozen in embarrassment and fear, looking at his Mom's face full of confusion and disappointment when she realized he had disobeyed her. Randy refused to answer any of her questions. He walked to the phone, called his Dad who lived across town, and packed his suitcase.

Randy believed his mother did not want him back, and he felt frightened and lonely. He did not know what to do, and he kept walking, hoping to find an answer.

When young people become angry or frustrated about household rules or parental unfairness, or wonder whether their parent really cares about them, they fight back in their own ways. Some escape to friends and parties to forget their problems for a few hours. Some sulk for hours in their room or listen to the stereo. Others find sports, reading, or hobbies to focus their energies and find pleasure outside their home. Many, like Randy, tell themselves that since they have two families, when life in one family becomes terrible, they can simply move in with the other.

In their anger with their at-home parent or stepparent, teens force a major crisis out of problems that could have been solved when the heat of the moment was past. Most teens who threaten to leave do not really want to leave home at all. They do want to hurt their at-home parent the way they feel that parent is hurting them. Some teens use the threat of leaving home as a weapon to gain what they want. Angry teens do want the troubling situation to improve, they do want their lives and the rules to be different. In their heart, however, most do not truly want to walk out the door.

Yet once the suitcases are packed and standing at the curb, young people have no graceful or face-saving way to retract their words. If they say they don't really want to leave, they just want to improve the situation, teens feel foolish and embarrassed. They want to be respected and taken seriously, and if they back down now, they appear weak and unsure of their own wishes.

When teens react to the moment's anger and declare their intention to live with their other natural parent, the at-home parent and stepparent must hear the real underlying concerns for an improved home life in *this* family. When tempers are high and nerves raw, family members should not make any important decisions. Wise parents and stepparents do not force their teens into a corner with sarcasm about helping them to empty their closets or taking suitcases down from the attic. Adults need to recognize the teens' anger and hurt and say that the family will make no decisions about living arrangements when everyone is upset. They should not take teens' threats at face value.

All concerned need time to cool down and talk calmly about the issues dividing them. After such talks, some rules change; others remain the same. In any case, the respect shown by both teens and adults in listening carefully to complaints and trying to understand what upsets all family members brings those involved a sense of closeness and trust that helps them work toward solving their problems together.

At the same time, parents and stepparents cannot allow their teens to "blackmail" them into backing down by always threatening to move out. Young people need to know that parents are ready to try to resolve the problems they all face. If a solution can be found in which everyone gains a little, fine. If, on the other hand, teens still do not like the household rules and refuse to obey them, and if the absent parent is truly willing to become the custodial parent, perhaps the teens should change residences. If they do, however, they must agree to remain for ten months to a year or more. Changing households in impossible situations is a possibility only when it is a real choice and commitment by all involved. Bouncing back and forth between two households whenever tempers flare does no one any good. Solving problems and living with one's decisions is a better way to learn responsibility.

*Problems With Sexuality*

Teens occasionally have more personal issues with which to deal in stepfamilies. Young people in single-parent families and in stepfamilies become aware of their parents as sexual persons. The single adult has close relationships with men or women. Teens watch their parent act coy and seductive, flirt, hold hands, and embrace a lover. The parent dresses more attractively to please dates and acts in ways the young people have never seen before. A remarried parent makes a big deal about privacy and spending time alone with the mate behind closed doors. Teens realize what is going on, but they feel uncomfortable about their parent's sexuality. This is not the parent they know.

These adolescents are becoming aware of themselves as sexual persons, too. Their bodies and emotions change as they mature physically. On the outside, they look like attractive young adults. Inside many teens feel like children. They want to understand this new aspect of their personality and body but they are not emotionally or socially ready to become sexually active. They are ready, however, for hugs, affection, tenderness, and love. They are ready to feel important and special as individuals. Watching their parent behave as a sexual person makes many teens feel pressured and uneasy. Teens are not yet comfortable with their own adult bodies or adult responses. Yet they see their experienced parents easily use this behavior, and they feel embarrassed at their own sexual ignorance. Some teens also think they are expected to act sexually mature and know they are not emotionally prepared to do so.

When teens feel themselves pushed out of the special relationship with their natural parent and notice the intimate physical closeness the adults share and enjoy, they feel angry and competitive. Some want to feel close and important again. If their stepparent used sexuality to gain their parent's interest and affection, teens sometimes see their own sexuality as a means of gaining similar interest and affection for themselves. If this approach works for their parent and stepparent, the young people reason, sexual activity should work for them, too.

Many teens begin acting seductively as they see or imagine their parent and stepparent acting, turning their charm either toward the adults at home or their own boyfriends or girlfriends. Wanting to understand their sexuality and seeing it as a tool to gain the closeness and affection they lost to their stepparent, many young people begin acting sexually before they are emotionally or socially prepared.

Adrienne, age sixteen, was such a confused young woman. She was playing a game with her mother and stepfather, but neither of the adults knew it.

Adrienne's father had divorced her Mom and moved away seven years earlier. He never visited and he never wrote. By the time her stepdad arrived, Adrienne did not care anymore about her Dad. She and Mom could manage fine without men in their lives. Suddenly her stepdad changed their lives when he married her Mom. Adrienne watched her Mom flirt, stand close to him, and put her arms around his waist so she could lean on his chest. Mom hung all over him, and he did not seem to mind.

At first, Adrienne felt left out of their twosome. She thought their behavior ridiculous, but she also was jealous of the affection Mom was receiving. So Adrienne decided to get some of her stepdad's affection, too. When he sat in the den, Adrienne would sit at his feet.

When he mowed the lawn, Adrienne would bring him iced tea and sit on the steps smiling and watching him work. She walked from her shower to her room wrapped only in a towel. She gave him long good-night kisses. Her stepdad liked Adrienne's attention and friendliness. He enjoyed having two good-looking women at home. He started asking her to go with him in the car on trips to the grocery store. He gave her attention that made her feel special and feminine.

Soon Adrienne's mother felt left out. She told Adrienne to show more modesty, cover up, and stop pestering her stepdad. Adrienne's Mom wondered if her daughter and husband were showing too much interest in each other, but Adrienne only laughed. She liked her stepdad's interest and was not about to give it up.

*Sexual Attraction Between Steprelatives.* Sexuality leads to other problems in stepfamilies. People find other people attractive and desirable. Individuals have certain looks and certain styles that others find appealing. In first families, mothers and fathers are proud that their sons and daughters look so attractive; they appreciate their teens' mature physical appearance. These attitudes are normal. A few parents may even wonder how their relationship with their teenagers would be different *if* they were seventeen years old again and meeting their children as strangers.

Most parents, however, do not find themselves at all sexually attracted to their teens. Parents admire them as sexual persons but do not *treat* them as sexual persons. Most parents looking at their teenagers remember how they were as tiny children learning to walk, starting school, or playing with toys.

What is more, the social taboo against sexual relations between parents and children, between sisters and brothers is so strong that most parents do not even let themselves think about their teenagers in that way. Parents are more comfortable thinking about their teenagers as young children, and brothers and sisters wonder why anyone in their right mind could even find their siblings attractive or exciting. If brothers or sisters do think of each other as physically attractive, they tell themselves they are crazy or they show great protectiveness toward the other, giving boyfriends and girlfriends a critical eye.

People consider the very idea of having sex with a son or

daughter, a brother or sister so wrong and disgusting that they feel guilty and ashamed even thinking about it. They do not understand that finding others attractive, even close relatives, is natural. Nevertheless, people have choices. They do not have to act on their thoughts. They can simply appreciate their children's or siblings' attractiveness without having to do anything about it and without blaming themselves for having such ideas. First families deal with sexuality by pretending it is not there or by recognizing it and leaving it alone.

Stepfamilies, however, change the rules about sexuality. Stepparents are not really related to their stepchildren. Stepbrothers and stepsisters are not really related to each other. They are legally but not biologically related. For some, the taboos against incest, or having sexual relations with close blood relatives, are not so strong. (Few states or countries have laws forbidding sexual relations between stepparents and stepchildren. If the young person is over the age of consent, usually eighteen years old, having sexual relations is adultery. If the child is a minor, the stepparent may be charged with child abuse.)

In addition, steprelatives have not usually known each other since infancy or as young children. They have not shared years of daily interaction. They do not look at the teenager and remember the toddler or the childhood illnesses or the annoying phases. They have not spent years becoming comfortable in each other's presence as natural fathers and mothers have done. Teens even complain that their parents treat them as if they were still children. Memories are strong, and many parents really do see their sixteen-year-olds as they were at eight.

That is not always the case with steprelatives. Here are full-grown young men and women, younger or fresher versions of their own new husband or wife. Without the social or moral stigma of incest weighing on their minds, and without the memories of teenagers as immature youngsters, a few stepparents feel strong physical attraction for their teenage stepchildren. For similar reasons, stepbrothers and stepsisters sometimes feel strong sexual attraction for one another.

Of course, most stepparents and stepsiblings never act on these thoughts, which they consider wrong. In addition, stepparents have a satisfying relationship with their mate and are not interested in their stepchildren as sexual persons.

Other stepparents who have known the stepchildren for years feel more as natural parents do, remembering the teenagers as youngsters. Aware that their stepchildren are physically attractive, they do not find them at all sexually exciting. Nevertheless, many worry about hugging or touching their stepchildren, afraid that the loving physical affection might be misunderstood by the young people or by others as sexual interest. These stepparents sometimes hold back their tenderness and are hesitant to show attention to their stepchildren.

Teenage stepchildren, themselves, sometimes feel strong physical attraction to a stepparent. The stepparent is a stranger, not like the old familiar parent whom they have known forever. The stepparent may be younger and more attractive than the absent parent. Furthermore, teenagers themselves are beginning to feel like sexual persons, and they are aware of a stepparent in ways their younger brothers and sisters are not. If teens feel competitive with their natural parent about winning the new adult's affection, they may encourage the stepparent's sexual feelings. They may wear tight or flimsy clothing or exercise in front of the stepparent to gain attention. This behavior, however, may not be at all exciting or stimulating. It is just a normal way of behaving in certain families, and no one thinks anything about it. The teens hug, kiss, and flirt outrageously with the stepparent. They do not want a sexual relationship; they just use sex as a way to gain the interest and attention they lack.

Teenagers may also feel attracted to their stepbrothers and stepsisters. These steprelatives may be classmates whom the teens liked at school even before they became related through marriage. Yet here they are, living closely together in the same house, sharing the bathroom and dinner table, passing each other in the halls wearing only nightclothes or underwear. The teens feel sexual attraction but also believe it is wrong to feel that way. They are "brothers" and "sisters" now, but in reality they are also attractive strangers. Privacy is important in all families, but even more so in stepfamilies with teenagers.

While stepparents, stepchildren, and stepsibs occasionally feel sexually aroused by each other, most fight against these feelings and thoughts. They think they are bad or sick for even having such thoughts. Suddenly they feel awkward and uncomfortable around each other. They want more privacy. They spend less time with each other. Easygoing relationships between stepparents and stepchildren and between stepbrothers and stepsisters become filled with tension. They fight bitterly with each other. They become overly critical and nasty with each other. They try to force themselves apart through anger and arguments to hide their real emotions, about which they feel so guilty. Arguments and criticism help them control their sexual feelings by burying them under more acceptable ones. Every look of fondness, every hug or kiss that used to tell each other how much they liked and appreciated each other now is threatening. They fear it signals the start of a sexual encounter. They are afraid to show genuine affection or tenderness toward one another because they fear these innocent, caring actions will lead to sex.

Even stepparents, stepchildren, and stepsibs who feel no sexual attraction whatever for each other suddenly fear their honest affection, tenderness, and caring will be misunderstood as sexual advances. The stepfamily that had been a loving and happy place becomes a stressful battleground when members feel sexual attraction for each other and the shame and guilt that come with it.

Sometimes the affection, however, is more than the persons want. Connie, age fifteen, arrived at the airport with two suitcases and $1.28 in her purse. She had not seen her father in eight years, but here she was, about to start living with him and her stepmother.

Connie was an attractive young women, cute and popular. She was cooperative at home and always helped her mother with cooking and cleaning. The problem was with her new stepfather. He was a hardworking man who took good care of her mother. He did not have much to say to Connie, but he enjoyed teasing her, playfully pulling her hair and flipping up her wide skirts.

Connie and her Mom did not think much about this, but Connie became uncomfortable when her stepdad began coming into her bedroom while she was resting. Sometimes he opened the door while she was dressing.

Suddenly, her stepfather started acting angry toward her, yelling all the time, saying ugly things about her and her boyfriend. Nothing Connie could do or say was right. Life at home became a nightmare. Finally, Connie's Mom called her ex-husband and asked him to help. So here she was, 1,500 miles from her mother and friends, about to start a new life with a father she hardly knew.

Sexual attraction between adults is normal. Sexual attraction between stepparents and near-adult stepchildren is normal. Sexual attraction between teenage stepbrothers and stepsisters is normal. Yet to act on these attractions is wrong and terribly destructive. Marriages are based on trust and keeping oneself for one's mate. Sexual relations between a stepparent and stepchild would violate the marriage, destroy trust between the adults, and end the family. The guilt and shame of the sexually involved persons would make them dislike themselves for acting so dishonestly and selfishly.

Sexual relations between stepbrothers and stepsisters break religious and moral laws against physical intimacy before marriage and break the trust shared by the stepparent and natural parent about how their children should relate as "brothers" and "sisters."

Natural parents can ease the situation when they recognize and understand the sexual pressures under which their stepfamily with teenagers lives. The parent should openly identify and discuss those pressures with the stepparent and the teens. Family members should avoid doing anything to make the situation worse. Privacy is a must. Stepparents and teens should not deliberately or accidentally tease each other by wearing skimpy clothing or by walking around the house half-dressed. They must close their bedroom door while dressing or lounging in their underwear. Bathroom doors should be shut while individuals attend to their personal needs.

Setting privacy rules risks making family members self-conscious and uncomfortable about sex. It risks making them unable to relax and enjoy each other's company. Discussing sexual attraction sometimes makes them so self-conscious that they become afraid to show any affection or tenderness toward each other. Awkwardness, discomfort, and holding back from each other create different strains on stepfamily relationships.

Fortunately, speaking one's sincere concerns and fears aloud and working to resolve them takes away their power to control us. Naming sexual attraction as a possible problem makes it easier for stepfamily members to decide not to act on these natural feelings. Often such discussions actually make the individuals feel less sexually attracted to each other. They clear the air, reminding everyone of their proper place in the stepfamily. Once again, stepfathers and stepmothers become parents and teenagers become children, each with their rightful place and appropriate relationships. No secret games are possible because everyone remembers who is off limits.

When stepfamily members remember and accept their proper relationships, the tensions ebb and they become more able to relax and relate to each other as they should. This can only help stepfamilies survive.

*Conclusion*

Adolescence is usually the most difficult time to start living in a stepfamily. With so many changes happening in their own lives and bodies, big changes at home beyond their control or liking take away the safety net for young people's experimenting with maturity outside.

Most teens are still dealing with losses from divorce or parent death. They still feel angry or sad, and they do not feel ready to trust relationships with another adult.

Teens are also building separate identities as individuals able to make decisions for themselves and wanting to spend time with friends. The last thing they want is family togetherness and a set of new rules and routines to tie them up at home. They have lasting ties to their natural parents and bitterly resent stepparents who try to take charge and tell them how to live their lives. When stepparents act like replacement parents and make teens' natural parents appear less than perfect or try to push the absent parents out of the teens' lives, teens explode with outraged protectiveness and loyalty toward their natural parents. In addition, teens' new sexuality brings extra feeling-charged issues into stepfamilies' lives.

Young people are also looking for reminders that they still have their parents' love. Many arguments come down to this: Do you still love me best? Yet this question is one that natural parents cannot answer without placing their stepfamilies, themselves, at risk.

# CHAPTER VIII

## A Troubled Stepfamily

Ron has been June's stepfather for three years, and he doesn't remember a time when he and June were not suspicious or resentful of each other.

Problems with stepfamilies often arise when the single parent begins dating. When Ron and June's mother, Susan, started going out together, both were divorced parents. Ron's young son, Todd, was living with his mother in another state. June, a preteen, was living with her mother. Still hurting from his divorce, Ron was not looking for a serious relationship with Susan. He made no effort to get to know June. He did not talk with her when he came to visit. He did not ask questions about her school life, her interests, or her friends. He did not sometimes invite June when he and Susan went to the movies or out for a pizza. June was just "Susan's kid," as far as Ron was concerned. She was part of the "package" but not a part that needed his attention.

June didn't like Ron from the start. She wondered if in some way he were the reason Susan and June's father had divorced. June did believe that Ron's involvement was keeping her mother and father from getting back together.

By the time Ron and Susan began to get serious about each other and think about marrying, the damage was done. June had bad feelings about Ron and his relationship with her mother. She did not like him and did not want him living in her home. She never told Ron so to his face, but her rudeness and cold behavior let him know how she felt.

Meanwhile, Ron's romance with Susan was taking all his time and energy. He still did not give June much thought. He told himself, "Once Susan and I are married, everything will fall into place. I don't have to do anything special now as far as June is concerned." He never sat down with June and shared his feelings and worries about their living together after he married Susan. He never asked about her feelings or thoughts. June got the unspoken message that Ron did not care about her.

Susan did not help the situation, either. She liked feeling attractive and was excited about her new romance with Ron. She wanted this new relationship to be special, two lovers so involved with each other that the rest of the world seems not to matter. Susan wanted a romance like the one she had before she was a parent. Not including her daughter in the tight circle she was creating with Ron felt like the right thing to do. When she did remember June, Susan did not know how to include her daughter in her relationship with Ron without taking away some of the "magic." Susan tried to keep her life in two parts: one part girlfriend, the other part mother.

*June's "Real" Father*

June's natural father also stirred June's angry feelings about Ron. Her father lived several hours' drive away, but he made no effort to see her for many months. He was deeply hurt by the divorce, and he thought involvement with his daughter would make the hurt even worse by reminding him of what he was missing. What is more, he did not like having to get Susan's permission to visit his own daughter. The custody settlement made it seem as if June were Susan's child and "belonged" to her; June was not his anymore. He felt out of control when he thought of June and Susan; he had lost his marriage and his family. He did not like to be reminded of his failure and loss, so he simply stayed away.

When June's father did write or phone, he promised her gifts and visits. June was excited about his calls, but when he did not keep his promises she was disappointed and confused. She asked herself,"What did I do wrong to make Dad hate me?"

Her father also blamed Ron for preventing Susan and him from trying to solve their problems and possibly remarrying. He fueled June's fantasy about having her first family get back together. Both June and her father blamed Ron for keeping their first family separated.

All this upset June greatly. She was angry with her father but afraid to have or express these "bad" feelings for fear of pushing him further away. Ron was there; her father was gone. She was already angry with Ron, so she focused all her angry feelings on him, even those that really belonged to her father. When he disappointed her, June blamed Ron. When something went right and her father did what he promised to do, he got the credit and Ron got the blame for doubting that he would follow through.

June acted cold toward Ron. She was rude and uncooperative. She would talk back, argue over anything, and go out of her way to do what he had asked her not to do. Ron thought school was important, so June let her grades drop. Ron wanted June to show respect to him and to her mother by using proper language; June started cursing at home. Ron asked June to take less time in the bathroom in the morning so he could get ready for work; June stalled and dallied fixing her hair and makeup. The more uncooperative June acted, the more Ron criticized her. He was angry and hurt and tried harder to control her. Then June did something that showed Ron he could not control her behavior. Ron's anger told June that she was right in believing he did not like her.

*Ron and Susan*

The tension between Ron and June created problems between him and Susan. They had never talked seriously about parenting while they were dating. Now it appeared that they had very different ideas about child-rearing. Ron was strict; Susan was more relaxed. When Ron saw June act in a way that he thought wrong, he told her to stop. Susan preferred to overlook things she did not want to see. If June left the family room a mess with clothes, books, curlers, and magazines, Ron wanted her to clean it now. Susan made excuses for her daughter and either let the room stay messy or cleaned it herself.

Susan had liked the idea of June's having an adult man at home when she married Ron. She thought Ron would help her make decisions about what was best for her daughter. She thought June needed a man's point of view as she grew into young womanhood. What Susan did not like, however, was having June and Ron bicker over everything. Susan did not like having to take sides between the two people she cared most about. She also felt protective toward June. She knew June missed living with her father and felt responsible for that hurt. Susan looked at Ron and felt that he was not sensitive enough to June's hurt. He had no right to be so strict with her daughter. When June yelled at Ron, "You can't tell me what to do. You're not my real father!" Susan silently agreed. Ron started receiving Susan's unspoken messages that she cared more about her daughter than about him.

*Ron and Todd*

Ron's young son, Todd, lived with Ron's ex-wife in a far-off city. He was only three years old at the time of the divorce, and Ron visited with him for several weeks at a time during winter and summer vacations.

They grew to know and care about each other to the extent possible given the distance between them. Ron knew that he was a "Disneyland dad" much of the time with Todd. They had so little time together that he wanted Todd to enjoy their visits. When Todd acted in ways of which he disapproved, Ron rarely said anything critical. With so little time together, he did not want to make Todd angry with him.

Ron started to wonder if there really were such a thing as "quality time," those moments when two people can share their deepest thoughts, feelings, dreams, and fears. When parent and child such as Ron and Todd have only brief times together, too often the moments are spent having *fun*, tending to avoid "housekeeping" items like schoolwork, grades, and health and making small talk to fill up the space between them. Quality time sometimes needs quantity time in which to occur. Parent and child need enough hours and weeks together to get beyond the small talk and to become comfortable and relaxed enough to let their real selves come through. Ron and Todd liked the weeks-long visits best because they could really know each other. During those visits, Ron even felt able to scold and correct Todd if he acted out of line.

Ron loved Todd very deeply. He cherished the special bond with his son. They shared that blood and emotional tie unique to parents and children. Living apart from his son saddened Ron, especially when he looked at the constant arguing of his life with his stepdaughter. It did not occur to him that June's father might have the same feelings about her that he did about Todd.

*The Cycle of Hurt*

Having a good relationship with his own son made it harder for Ron to be patient with June. The more he remembered Todd's loving and caring for him, the more Ron resented living with an uncaring and mean-tempered stepchild. The more lack of concern June showed for Ron's wishes, the stricter he wanted to be with her. He wanted to show her who was in control. Ron told himself that people make sacrifices and bend for people they care about. If June cared about him she would at least meet him halfway. He believed that June did not care about his feelings as Todd did. June wouldn't listen to his advice or accept his discipline the way Todd did. At least if Todd misbehaved he would just be immature or irresponsible; his love and respect for Ron were never in doubt. When June misbehaved, however, she was immature, irresponsible, and spiteful, too.

Ron forgot that Todd was not an angel or a perfect child and that he occasionally needed correcting. Ron also forgot to think about how June felt. June could also tell herself that if Ron really cared about her, he would be more sensitive and considerate. In addition, Ron saw June as part of Susan. He told himself that if Susan really loved him June would not act so badly. He held Susan responsible for June's behavior and felt hurt that Susan did not put a stop to it. Instead, the cycle of hurt pushed Ron, June, and Susan farther away from one another.

Ron hated to go home after work. He hated the nastiness, the constant arguing, and the lack of warmth between himself and his stepdaughter. More and more, he and Susan were arguing and angry with each other, too. He felt like the "odd man out." Every day he had to fight in his own home. It was draining him. Even his work was affected. Ron felt too tired to maintain the standards of excellence he prized at the office. He saw himself giving in, letting go, and compromising about issues that he would have stood up for before. He no longer respected his own efforts at home or at work. He was losing respect for himself as a parent, as a husband, and as a professional. Ron was desperately unhappy and plain worn out. Although he and Susan started seeing a professional family therapist, he knew he could not put up with a bad and worsening situation much longer. After all, he had already been through one divorce. A second would bring few surprises.

*Mistakes in This Stepfamily*

This is a troubled stepfamily. It may sound like many stepfamilies or it may seem very different. Like many stepfamilies, its members are making basic mistakes in the ways they relate to each other.

*Lack of communication.* People in this stepfamily are not talking openly and caringly to each other about what they see, what they need, and how they might make family life better. Ron and June did not communicate in words when they first met. Ron did not try to get to know June as a person while he was dating her mother. The unspoken message to June was that Ron did not care about her. She was right. After the marriage, she started acting in ways to give Ron the same message. Neither of them tried to use words to make satisfying contact.

Ron and Susan also showed a lack of communication from the start of their serious relationship. They did not discuss parenting. They did not share their views about household rules or discipline. They ignored the topic and only began to argue about how each thought the other should act after the problems had begun. Not thinking about troubling issues does not make them go away. Relationships don't take care of themselves.

People in stepfamilies need to reach out to each other from the start to really know one another. They need to talk and listen to each other's words and each other's behaviors. If one person acts in ways that hurt the other, the behavior should be brought into the open and talked about. Identifying problems is the first step to solving them. On the other hand, hurt feelings not addressed lead to more hurtful behavior and a cycle of mutual hurt.

*Lack of Sensitivity to Others' Feelings.* Ron, June, and Susan all showed a lack of caring about the feelings of the others in their stepfamily. Each played a role, stepfather, stepdaughter, mother/wife, and did not try to relate to the unique persons inside the other roles. From the first days, June was a person who had lost her family and her father and was now losing her mother's single-parent attention. She needed to know for sure that her mother still loved her, but Ron acted as if she were not there. Ron also experienced loss of his own family and young son, and he made a big mistake with June, but June kept trying to hurt him as much as she felt he was hurting her. June blamed Ron. Ron blamed June and Susan. Susan started blaming June but then began to blame Ron for their troubled family. Each person was so involved with his or her own disappointment and frustration that no one could see or care about the same emotions in the others. Family members try to protect themselves by fighting back, by hurting as they have been hurt.

*Discomfort About the Absent Parent.* This stepfamily had two absent parents. June's father was one, and Ron resented his continued involvement with June and Susan. Ron had June's anger, and the absent father had her love and loyalty.

Ron was also an absent parent to his son. He missed Todd and wished he could be there for his growing-up years. The worse time he had with June, the more Ron idealized Todd and used that fantasy to feel more bitter toward the problems in his stepfamily.

*The Noncustodial Parent's Feelings.* Parents who do not receive custody of their children and see them only on a part-time basis often feel disappointed and embarrassed. Many noncustodial parents, like Ron, want to play an important role in their children's lives. They also feel that having their children live with the other parent makes them look like poor parents. Their self-esteem suffers. They are afraid they and their children will slowly drift apart and become strangers. They wonder whether the custodial parent will say nasty things about them or do things to make the children not want to visit. When children do visit, they do not know the house rules, they do not have all their own toys and clothing, and they do not have many neighborhood friends. Discipline becomes a problem and strains the ties between parent and child.

Having long visits when Ron and Todd could really act like father and son, not just host and guest, would enable them to know and love each other better. If Ron could feel like a father to Todd, he would be a more flexible and caring stepfather to June.

*Lack of Flexibility.* Stepfamily members need to show flexibility. They need flexibility toward their roles. For instance, they do not have to act as they think a "father" or "mother" or "child" is supposed to act. They need to be persons first. With a teenager, a stepfamily is wise to let the natural parent do the parenting and allow the stepparent to gradually build a relationship with the young person as an interested adult friend.

Stepfamily members need flexibility about who is a member of the family. Absent parents are still members of the stepfamily. As long as absent parents continue to have relationship with their children and ex-spouses, their presence is a fact of life. Pretending or wishing this were not so, or being angry with their hold over the family members' love and loyalty will not change what is. Extended family and certain friends from first families may also be part of the stepfamily.

Stepfamily members need flexibility about changes in their lifestyles. New routines and new rules are part of coming together as a stepfamily, and members need flexibility to give and take. For a while everyone may be uncomfortable, but sooner or later all will get used to the new ways. Flexibility about rules and routines reminds us that there is not only one right way to do most things. This is a learning time. Some ways are better, and some are simply different. Some are worse. Flexibility and goodwill by all members will in time help decide which rules and routines suit them and which need change.

Flexibility is also necessary when dealing with other people. People make mistakes. Mistakes are uncomfortable for the doer and for the receiver. Trying to fight back or get even with stepfamily members for their errors will only set up a cycle of hurt that leaves no winners. Flexibility means that stepfamily members need to communicate their needs, name the annoying behavior, listen to the other family member's point of view, try again, and forgive the other person. Flexibility means patience, kindness, communication, goodwill, and forgiveness.

Be realistic! Learning to live together in a happy family takes time and practice. Patience, kindness, communication, goodwill, and forgiveness are not easy virtues, but they are useful ones for building satisfying stepfamilies.

# CHAPTER IX

## When One Parent Is Gay

Most children see and hear their parents argue from time to time. Parents disagree about money, discipline, and relatives, but they usually keep the most personal matters away from the children. Children seldom know about sexual or loyalty problems that are upsetting their parents. That is as it should be; such matters belong only to the parents.

When parents separate or divorce, however, children hear or discover new information about them. Sometimes children learn that one of their parents is gay, is sexually attracted to a person of the same sex. Children may learn this fact directly from the gay parent who tries to explain the reasons for the divorce. They may learn it from their straight parent, who cites the other parent's homosexuality as the reason. Children may learn the fact from gossip and teasing at school, in the neighborhood, or at family events.

### Parents Can Be Gay

No one knows for sure why some people are attracted to persons of the same sex. Parents can be gay. These persons are attracted to persons of both sexes, and they probably have been for a long time. When they were growing up, they learned about their own attraction to other men or women. These feelings never disappeared, but they knew that society considered such a physical attraction to a member of the same sex to be wrong.

For preteens, "crushes" on other boys or girls are common and a normal and healthy part of growing up. Most teens outgrow crushes as they become more mature physically and emotionally and start making ties with members of the opposite sex. Such crushes are not the same as being gay.

Although it is against the law to discriminate against gay persons, many people have strong feelings against homosexuality. The AIDS epidemic of the 1980s and 1990s has added to the anger many people feel toward homosexuals. When the AIDS disease first came to public attention, gay men were among the first groups to become sick. As a result, AIDS became linked to gays as if they had caused the epidemic instead of being its victims.

Knowing how poorly gays are viewed, young people who want others to think well of them try to act in the "right" ways. For gay parents, their attraction to both men and women helped them decide to act on their attraction to the opposite sex because that was the "right" way. Many bisexuals fell in love with and married persons of the opposite sex and had families.

When bisexual persons marry, they try to make the marriage a good one. They do whatever it takes to be a real partner. Sometimes they tell their spouse that they are bisexual, and they agree not to act on those feelings because the marriage and family are too important to risk. Many times bisexual husbands or wives do not tell their spouse because they believe that such information is too personal to share. Usually, therefore, husbands and wives do not know it when their spouse and their children's parent is gay.

Sometimes gay husbands or wives can live happily in a traditional marriage. They keep those feelings and thoughts to themselves. For others, ignoring or denying the feelings becomes too difficult. They want to be themselves. They believe that denying those feelings is denying an important part of who they are. No matter how much they love their spouse and children, they feel that they are living a lie. They are willing to risk their family's happiness and anger. When a parent decides to act openly on gay feelings, he or she must leave the marriage to live a different type of life. Divorce results.

*Telling the Children*

Marriages break up for many reasons. Wanting to lead a gay lifestyle is one reason for divorce. A gay parent, however, cannot stop being a parent. Most gay parents love their children deeply, as do other parents. Wanting to stop living in a heterosexual marriage does not mean wanting to stop being a parent. The sexual role and the parental role are very different and entirely separate.

Telling children that their parents are divorcing is very difficult. Children do not need to know the intimate details that led to the divorce. Children also do not want to know about the parents' sexual behavior. They need only to know that although the husband and wife are divorcing each other, they are not divorcing their children. The parents will keep on being their parents, will keep on loving and taking care of them.

Many children never learn than one parent is gay. On the other hand, some children hear about it in offhand ways through gossip or teasing. Some overhear their parents talking about the matter. In a few cases one parent comes right out and tells the child that one parent is gay.

When children learn about a parent's gay preference in a calm, accepting way that places no blame, they are more likely to keep their loving relationship with both parents after the divorce. If children learn about the gay issue in an angry, blaming, hurtful way they will probably feel the need to choose one parent over the other. Parents' own feelings about the matter and whether they tell or don't tell the children has a large impact on whether the children and the gay parent are able to keep their ties after the divorce.

However children learn that their parent is gay, those old enough to understand what it means are stunned. They wonder how it can be true, and for a while they pretend it is not so. Many become very angry at their gay parent, believing that being gay caused the divorce. They also are aware of the social disapproval of homosexuality, and that makes their gay parent seem "different." To children, different often seems bad. That intensifies the angry feelings. These children also feel hurt and very sad.

Some children wonder whether having a gay parent means that they will grow up to be gay. Being gay is not hereditary and is not contagious. Knowing that will help children accept their gay parent without fear of its "rubbing off."

The feelings of shock, anger, and hurt go away in time if the parents accept their divorce without bitterness and if they help the children realize that both parents still love them and will care for them. All children started life in a family in which a mother and father loved each other and together created a child. Even when the husband and wife can no longer share a marriage, they still love their children. That is the message that children need to hear if they are to keep strong ties with both their parents.

*Dealing with Friends*

Not all children know that a parent is gay. Wise parents keep their intimate lives separate from their lives as parents. Unfortunately, however, rumors or facts about one parent's gay nature may spread. Parents talk to friends or relatives, who in turn talk to husbands, wives, and friends. Children overhear adults talking. Before too long, outsiders may suspect or know the situation even before the person's own children.

It is painful to children for classmates and friends to tease them about a gay parent. They may hear remarks about their "gay Dad" or "dyke Mom." It is especially unpleasant and confusing when the children themselves do not know the truth. They are very embarrassed when others know such personal information about their parents. Children do not want anyone to think ill of their parents, and they feel ashamed when outsiders suspect or know the truth. They worry that other children will stop liking them.

Ignoring mean comments from others is difficult. Children feel embarrassed, angry, hurt, and confused when they are teased. When the subject of the teasing is so very personal and about their parent, they are torn between keeping their friends and protecting their parent. The teasing stops sooner if children either walk away without a word and without showing hurt, or face it with a confident, "That's none of your business."

Parents can help when they separate and divorce without encouraging children to feel angry and ashamed of their other parent. Parents also help children when they keep their personal lives private and share them only with clergy or marriage counselors.

*Coping with a Gay Stepparent*

Most divorced parents try to keep their personal lives separate from their lives as parents. Children are loyal to their natural parents and do not like outsiders coming between them, even when the parents are divorced. Most children believe that even divorced parents belong together. As a result, introducing children to a parent's new boyfriend or girlfriend is difficult for everyone.

When one parent is gay, the situation becomes even more difficult. Not only is the parent's boyfriend or girlfriend an outsider, but he or she is also "the wrong sex." The child has to face not only the sadness of divorce but also the sadness of a society that says the gay parent is bad. That is a lot of disapproval to overcome for any child who wishes to stay close to a gay parent.

What the other parent says about the gay parent makes a big difference in the way the child treats the gay parent's friends. Hearing from one parent how bad, how "sick," how "immoral" the gay parent is, the child is likely to go along with that judgment. This child is likely to behave badly towards the gay parent and his or her friends, perhaps even refusing to visit the gay parent. If the child is told that the gay parent is not a bad person but one who has different needs and who is still a loving parent, the child is more willing to accept the situation.

Children cannot really have a gay stepparent, because in this country homosexuals cannot legally marry. Children sometimes do meet and even visit or live with the gay parent's friends or lovers. It is not important that they know the exact relationship between the friend and the parent. The parental role should be as separate as possible from the gay parent's personal relationships.

As in most stepfamily situations, however, the gay adult is wise to allow the natural parent to set rules and enforce discipline. Children strongly resent scolding, nagging, or punishing by anyone other than the natural parent. If the gay parent's friends want to have a relationship with the children, they do better when they get to know the children slowly, as caring adults to young persons, while they join in games, sports, family dinners, or household chores. Like any relationship, it takes time, shared experiences, and a mutual desire for trust and understanding.

# CHAPTER X

## Coping with Stepfamilies

Remarriage and stepfamilies bring many changes. Family members have new relationships to make and new roles to fill. Rules and routines change. Life at home is different from how it used to be. What is more, stepfamilies do not start on blank pages of new books. Many chapters with other people and other experiences have already been written. All people remember their first family, and many wish to keep active ties to absent parents and relatives. They want to keep familiar possessions such as houses, favorite toys, old pictures, and special clothing as reminders of good times and reminders of who they are.

In stepfamilies, some members feel sad about their losses. Others feel excited about their gains. Some make decisions about living arrangements. Others reluctantly go along with those decisions. Some want to make family members feel like a whole family immediately. Others hold back, keeping ties to the past and testing to see if they can really trust this new arrangement and the new people in it. Everyone wonders where they belong and how they fit together.

Stepfamilies are complicated. Members bring their own histories, personalities, and needs to the group. Often they find themselves in conflict with other members who have very different histories, personalities, and needs. If family members can understand the unique issues that a stepfamily creates and show one another respect, patience, and sensitivity as they work through those issues, a stepfamily can become a happy and satisfying place to live.

Not all stepfamilies have problems. Some easily and happily fit together. Reviewing the previous chapters about stepfamilies helps alert family members to the realities with which they live. Children and adults alike aid each other's adjustments when they act with awareness of these concerns.

*Understand Your Losses*

Young people in stepfamilies have gone through tremendous losses. They have lost the security of their first family. They feel they can no longer depend on people to keep loving each other. They cannot depend on adults' successfully solving their problems by staying together. The world no longer is predictable or safe. Anything can and often does happen. While people may not like these changes, wishing them away does not put life back the way it was. Letting go of the old ways of living and seeing things, however, is hard.

Young people in stepfamilies, having lost their first family, feel as if they have also lost their single parents. One parent lives somewhere else and the other seems too involved with his or her new spouse. The younger the children, except for babies who are too young to tell people apart, the more they miss their absent parent's involvement in their life. Young people also miss the special place they held in their single-parent family. They are no longer their parent's best friend, "man of the house," or "little homemaker." Many now stop sleeping in their single parent's bedroom and move into their own room. Some now share their personal space with stepbrothers or stepsisters. Some young people in stepfamilies move into new homes, attend new schools, and shop at new stores in new neighborhoods. They lose their old friends, teachers, and familiar surroundings. For the first few months of stepfamily life, everything seems different and nothing feels comfortable.

Finally, a stepfamily means losing dreams of bringing their natural parents back together. One or both parents have remarried. Even years after divorce or death, many children still want more than anything to put their first family back together. Letting go of this comforting dream feels like the biggest loss of all.

When young people experience loss, they become sad or angry, or both. They did not ask for these changes. They did not want these new people in their family or these new living arrangements. Feeling sad or angry makes young people want to strike out at their parent, stepparent, or stepsibs to hurt them the way they believe these others have hurt them. Sometimes young people feel sad or angry without knowing why. They are not really annoyed with their stepfamily or its members; nevertheless, those people receive the brunt of these angry feelings.

Feeling so many losses makes young people hold back from their new family. They do not want to cooperate nor feel any liking for the newcomers. Some unhappy young people want to stay in their room, coming out only to eat or go to the bathroom and not talking to anyone. Others want to stay away from home as much as possible, engaging in school activities or visiting friends.

Just when remarried parents feel happiest about finding a new mate, many young people have never felt more miserable or distrustful. If parents and children can understand the many losses the young people are experiencing, they can be more patient with each other and with themselves. Grieving takes time. It cannot be rushed with lectures on how happy they all will be now that they belong to a family again.

Young people need to feel sad or angry to let go of their old ideas and old habits and gradually accept the way things are. If parent and stepparent believe that the sadness or anger means only hate for the new adults or the family situation, they miss the point. It is not wise to take young people's unhappiness personally when many other reasons exist for their bad moods. When adults believe the young people are criticizing their remarriage, they feel they need to prove their choice correct. Then family arguments and tensions increase. That in turn tells the grieving young people they were right to be upset in the first place. This stepfamily is a bad idea. All everyone does is fight and complain. And the conflict intensifies still more.

Only time to feel angry or sad and chances to share pleasant activities with stepfamily members prove to young people that stepfamily life can be satisfying.

*Belonging to Two Families Is Okay*

Children in stepfamilies belong to two families. They live day-to-day with one family, their stepfamily, but in their heart and mind they belong to their absent parent's family, too. They may even be active parts of a second stepfamily when they visit their absent parent and new stepparent. In their first family everyone knew where he belonged. Belonging to two families confuses young people because the lines of who fits where and with whom are unclear. Nevertheless, belonging to two families in these situations is natural and okay. Simply because it is different from life in a first family does not mean it is wrong.

Occasionally, parents have more problems with this matter than do their children. Parents divorce each other. Ex-spouses become part of the past, forgotten or ignored. Children, however, do not divorce their parents. Even when parents live elsewhere, the emotional and legal ties remain. The relationship between children and absent parent remains as strong and as vital as the persons involved want to keep it. Parents failed to make their first marriage succeed, but children have not failed. They have not made mistakes to feel guilty about. They do not have to pretend their relationship with their absent parent does not exist. Young people still belong with both parents even after the parents no longer belong with each other.

Parents make problems for their children when they ask them to spy on their other parent. Sometimes parents use young people to deliver messages to the ex-spouse: The child-support checks are not arriving on time or the child returned home after the last visit with a stomachache from eating too much junk food.

Without thinking, parents put children in the middle where they cannot make one parent happy without hurting the other. Young people so placed in the middle can get themselves off the hot spot by refusing to carry out such requests. Mom's home is her home. Dad's home is his home. Let parents talk directly to each other and fight their own battles. If parents want information about each other, let them have the courage to ask directly rather than turning the young people into tattletales. Young people in this spot should tell their parents to stop using them unfairly. They need to be able to enjoy their times with each parent, not feel unhappy playing the traitor.

When divorced parents realize their children's need to belong to both parents, they help them feel comfortable doing what they want most to do. Most young people wish to keep the ties with their absent parent but do not want to hurt or disappoint their custodial parent. When ex-spouses cooperate about visiting schedules, child-support payments, and other issues that concern their children, the young people feel free to keep loving both parents and to belong to both families. When young people can keep the satisfying bonds with their absent parent, they are more likely to adjust to their stepfamily as well. Divided loyalties lessen as young people realize they do not have to select one parent over the other, or a natural parent over a stepparent. People who want to love always have enough love to go around.

People differ, and no two relationships are the same. Younger children express more interest than teenagers in seeing their absent parent often. On the other hand, some young people do not really like or trust their absent parent, who has disappointed them too often, broken too many promises, acted unfairly or uncaringly too often. Without feeling a loyalty conflict between parents or between absent parent and stepparent, the young people, usually teens, have maturely decided they no longer trust or respect the absent parents enough to continue pretending they have a good relationship. The young people need to think about what they want from their absent parent in the future. Perhaps they want nothing but to be left alone to live their life according to their own values, beliefs, and goals.

Similarly, no two households are alike. Rules and routines are strict in one home, looser in the other. Some families eat at 5 p.m., others dine at 7. These, too, represent details to work out. Different rules and routines in their two families are small matters compared to keeping strong emotional ties. Young people express confusion at first about these details, but they adjust. Households have unique personalities, just as people do, and they make possible richer experiences and alternative ways of solving problems. Again, differences between two homes are not wrong, merely different.

*Children Need Not Love Their Stepparent (and Vice Versa)*

Sometimes stepparents and children make a big mistake. They want so much to create a happy family that they expect to love one another instantly. When this love does not happen, each feels disappointed, hurt, and angry, cheated out of something he really wants.

Young people already have two parents whom they love. Simply because an adult has the title "stepparent" does not mean young people feel the same affection, duty, or appreciation they feel for a natural parent. In fact, considering all the losses young people have recently experienced, few are ready to welcome the stepparent into their home at all, let alone trust or love that person.

Young people and stepparents are really strangers to each other, even if they knew one another before the wedding. They need chances to know each other as individuals, to learn each other's personalities, moods, values, and ways of doing things. They need to live together, share good times, and solve problems together. Liking each other takes time. Respect takes longer. Love, if ever, takes longer still.

In a way, living with stepparents brings many opportunities not always possible in first families with two natural parents. Parents often take their children for granted. They love their sons and daughters, or course, but they do not always know them as unique people with their own ideas, values, and interests. They know one another well from years of living together. They know what foods the others prefer, what clothing styles the others like, what illnesses the others have suffered. Yet all people grow and change. They have new experiences that cause them to view themselves and their world in different ways. Too often, life at home goes on in the regular routine, day after day, without taking opportunities really to listen to one another's ideas, dreams, or fears. People often know their friends better than they know their own family members. They see friends as people with different histories, preferences, beliefs, and interests. They want to know their friends better, so they make time to do so. Meanwhile, they assume they already know their own family members and do not always make the time to know them better.

Stepparents and stepchildren, too, are strangers. When they accept this fact, they can deliberately work to know each other better. Although they may never become like natural parent and children, they can become close, caring, and trusted friends with whom to share both fun times and troubled ones. Stepparents and stepchildren have much to offer each other when they step outside their family roles and relate instead as interested persons.

Calling a stepparent "your new Dad" or "your new Mom" forces young people into a no-win situation. Young people do not want to give up their natural parent, and they suspect that is exactly what the adults want them to do. If they pretend their stepparent is a "new parent," youngsters feel disloyal to their absent parent.

On the other hand, if young people refuse to make a relationship with their stepparent, they know they are hurting their remarried parent. All would do better to think of a stepparent as an "additional parent" or adult friend, not as a substitute or replacement parent. Nobody replaces anyone. No one assumes the stepparent and children will love each other. The married adults love each other, and that is enough for now. Other relationships grow slowly. All a stepparent and stepchildren can fairly expect from each other is fairness, patience, and politeness.

## Stepfamilies Need Not Look and Feel Like "First" Families

Stepfamilies *are* real families. They are not, however, first families. For this, no one need apologize, because all families are as different as the persons and experiences that create them.

Families throughout history have changed to meet the needs of the persons and social conditions creating them. Stepfamilies simply represent another style. Stepfamilies in themselves are not better or worse than any other form of family. They are as satisfying and as meaningful as their members make them.

In stepfamilies, some members have different last names. This may be confusing at times, but it need not be a problem. In stepfamilies, members have separate past experiences from previous families. Even in first families, members have separate experiences at work, at school, or with friends, yet no one feels awkward about that. In stepfamilies, young people belong to two households with their separated natural parents. The family boundaries are more open and flexible in stepfamilies to permit members to enter and leave. This is not unlike earlier families when mothers, fathers, children, grandparents, aunts, uncles, and cousins lived and worked together. It is not unlike first families in which relatives visit each other. In extended or large families, members do what they can to make the whole family thrive, and no one feels awkward about that.

Many ways to be a family exist to meet individual and societal needs. To think otherwise makes stepfamily members feel second-best. It makes them feel like failures who need to apologize for being themselves. Believing in one right type of family forces members into relationships that do not fit, into denying ties that do fit, and into pretending feelings they do not have. When honest feelings come through, everyone becomes upset because they believe they will look like failures again. Pretending one right type of family exists is not only a wrong idea; it is a bad idea because it pressures members to play a hurtful, dishonest game.

Stepfamily members show great awareness of their differences from first families. They think these differences are bad. Family members are no longer mother-father-children in a tight little circle. They have not married once and lived happily ever after. They did not walk directly from their parents' home into their married home with white gown, bridesmaids, orange blossoms, and innocent hopes for the future. Because stepfamily members come together after hurts, mistakes, and disappointments, they sometimes need to prove themselves successful at marriage. They want to erase past errors, forget past disappointments, and pretend they are starting over with a blank slate. That is why stepfamily members try to appear like first families. They want the titles "Mom" and "Dad." They want love, obedience, and respect from their children. They want to shut the front door to all outsiders. They want neighbors and the larger community to think of them as a "real" family rather than as something less.

Stepfamilies do start over, but they cannot forget or deny the past. The past happened, and persons can do better next time only when they learn from their mistakes. In addition, parents' pasts are the children's present. Absent parents play important roles in stepfamilies.

Something "else" is not necessarily something "less." When stepfamilies accept their special qualities instead of pretending to be some other form of family, all members have much to gain. When stepfamily members show true happiness with their complex relationships and complicated households, any doubting outsiders will have to do the same.

*Be Patient With Change*

Stepfamily life means many changes. New and unfamiliar people enter the family and new relationships begin. Children belong to two households, each with its own rules of conduct. Children sometimes move into new neighborhoods, attend new schools, with new teachers and new classmates. Hundreds of details shift, and little seems as comfortable as it used to be.

Changes upset everyone. Even pleasant changes take getting used to. Letting go of old ways and old habits is not easy. The old ways worked well, and no one promises the changes will bring happiness. With so many hurts in the past and so many new relationships, rules, and routines with which to become comfortable, no wonder young people dig in their heels and do not want to cooperate. They already feel angry and distrustful, yet now even more familiar ways are being taken away.

At first, it is difficult to see where the changes lead. Do rules change for the sake of showing who is boss or to find better ways of solving problems in daily life? Are the new rules and routines really more effective or are they merely different? Do new relationships with stepparents and stepbrothers and sisters make people happier, or are they simply part of the larger package? Lots of questions remain unanswered.

Parents, stepparents, and children do well to keep changes to a minimum. Living closely with strangers itself brings enough adjustments and compromises. Adding extra rules simply so stepparents can prove "I am here!" is not necessary or helpful. Unnecessary changes create more chances for friction and arguments. Extra rules and routines become problems and distract family members from the more important task: learning to relate to each other. When young people and adults argue about mealtimes, curfews, or dress codes, they cannot quietly learn about the newcomers as people worth knowing and liking. All family members learn, instead, who has the power and who must give in.

Furthermore, people have their own ways of doing things. One approach may reflect personal habits and tastes that are not better, only different. When young people have occasions to observe new ways of handling the same issues, they gain choices. Viewing alternatives allows them to select the approach that best suits them and the problem. Choices permit resourcefulness. Learning new ways of doing things also builds flexibility. An attitude that allows for many "right" answers gives individuals a wider range of options with which to respond. Watching others solve problems in different ways permits young people to select the best solutions rather than use the only choices they know. It allows them to meet novel situations with greater confidence and greater success.

Stepfamilies bring changes, and they also bring opportunities for personal growth. Rather than viewing adjustments in rules and relationships as nuisances, members who view them as chances to meet interesting people and learn more ways of viewing the world find stepfamilies exciting and satisfying places to live.

The major issues in stepfamilies include developing the ability to give and take. Everyone gives in on some issues and gets what he wants on others. It means allowing the adults to build strong bonds with each other that will let them feel good about themselves as mates and as parents. It means recognizing members as separate individuals with their own abilities, interests, and needs. It means allowing room for members to grow, to make mistakes, and to learn from their errors. These issues all families, first families as well as stepfamilies, share.

*See Parents and Stepparents as Individuals*

To many young people, adults appear to be all-powerful. Adults seem to have all the answers, to know how to handle confusing situations. Adults can scold, spank, reward, and punish. They set and enforce rules for young people. Adults have information, skills, money, and freedom to act. Young people depend on adults to give them food, clothing, home, and safety.

As young people grow older and gain more skills and information, they begin to see adults in a different way. They find that adults do not have all the answers. Adults can be confused and make mistakes. Maturing young people begin to see their parents and stepparents as people with their own strengths and weaknesses, their own doubts and fears. Parents and stepparents no longer appear all-wise or all-powerful; they are simply people doing the best they can to make their way in the world just as young people are doing. Certainly adults have more years of making decisions and handling situations, but young people are also learning. As young people mature, they, too, make more and more good choices and act effectively on their own.

When young people come to view their parents as human beings, several things happen. First, young people forgive their parents for making mistakes. Anyone can make poor decisions. Everyone has choices and must live with the results of his actions. Wrong choices make individuals unhappy. They must then look at the situation, see what makes them unhappy, and decide how to improve their lives.

Parents divorce as a way to improve their lives. It is their solution to very troubling problems in their marriage. Parents remarry to make their own lives, and hopefully their children's lives, happier. They do not deliberately set out to make themselves or their children miserable or afraid.

When young people view their parents and stepparents as people, they stop being so angry and stop blaming the adults for every sadness they feel. Parents and stepparents are people with much to learn and who do the best they can. All young people can hope is that adults in their lives learn from their errors and do not make the same mistakes twice.

Young people separating from their families want the freedom to act on their own, to make their own decisions and act on them. They want chances to succeed or fail on their own. If they get what they want, they gain confidence in their ability to make good choices. If they fail, they want to pick themselves up, learn from their mistakes, and do better next time. Parents and stepparents deserve the same consideration.

Next, when young people see parents and stepparents as real people, they make chances to know the adults as individuals. The adults have ideas, values, and experiences worth sharing. They have interests and hobbies that could give the young people pleasure. Adults have worries, concerns, and doubts just as young people do, which when quietly discussed together can build supportive bonds between them as well as offer possible answers to puzzling questions.

When people treat each other as separate and unique individuals, they slowly create strong ties based on respect, understanding, and caring for each other. They can become more like friends who genuinely know and like each other instead of playing the impersonal roles of breadwinner, housekeeper, and children.

Finally, when young people view parents and stepparents as flesh and blood persons, they have already begun the process of emotionally separating from their families. They see their parents and stepparents as apart from themselves. The adults' problems are their problems, not the young people's. The adults' mistakes are their mistakes, not the young people's.

When this happens, young people feel freer to look at themselves as unique individuals without fearing to repeat the adults' errors in their own lives. Young people look for their personal abilities and interests. They look to see what truly matters to them, choose what goals they will pursue, and decide what values they want to live by. Looking at adults in these ways helps young people take the first steps toward their own independence, responsibility, and maturity.

When young people understand and accept their parents and stepparents as individuals, young people are better able to understand and accept themselves. From this position, decisions that make their own lives more satisfying, enjoyable, and meaningful become possible.

*Talk It Out*

People come to stepfamilies with many ideas about what they want to happen or what they expect to happen. Some expect to love the newcomers; others expect to hate them. Some stepparents want to take active parenting roles with their spouse's children; others prefer to step back and let the natural parent take charge of the young people. Some children expect to keep strong ties with their absent parent while others fear their stepfamily will force them to drop those ties.

Countless thoughts about what their stepfamilies will be like affect the ways individuals interact with each other. When people expect events to occur in certain ways and others with whom they live expect different outcomes, each faces frustrations, disappointments, and anger. Arguments and bad feelings result.

It is normal to wonder how life will be in a stepfamily. Stepparent, natural parent, and young people all have their own ideas about it, and those ideas govern the way they act with each other. Too often, those ideas remain private and unspoken. No one understands the others' frame of mind or goals for their new family. So many changes, so many silent wishes and fears bring many chances to create conflict.

Stepfamilies do not have the years of courtship, marriage, and childbirth to slowly grow and adjust to individual members. All at once, a full-blown family exists. To prevent extra confusion and disappointments, stepfamilies need to make frequent chances for all members to express their thoughts and goals. Members need to sit down regularly and voice their wishes, hopes, and concerns so that all may know the others' desires for family living. They can hear where they agree and where they disagree. Members can all decide how to live together through cooperation and compromise and respect for each others' feelings.

Stepfamily members need to discuss what type of family they want. Do they want traditional roles of father as breadwinner, mother remaining home? Do they prefer more flexible roles with both adults working outside the home and both taking on housekeeping jobs? What rules and routines should the stepfamily keep, and what new ones should it adopt? What about chores, curfews, meals, and bathroom use? What needs to be shared and what needs to remain private? Making these points clear helps stepfamilies work together without hard feelings born of unmet, unspoken wishes.

Stepparents and spouses need to decide openly and honestly about discipline. Does the stepparent want to play an active part in disciplining stepchildren or prefer for the natural parent to take over that duty? Does the natural parent really want the spouse to take parenting responsibilities? Will the natural parent strongly and visibly support the stepparent who wants to "parent" the stepchildren? What behavior is okay for the young people, and what is not proper? How was discipline handled before, and what should be continued? What limits and rules now need to be defined, understood, and maintained? Clarifying these issues prevents misunderstanding, crossed signals, and unnecessary friction.

Stepfamilies need to talk openly about deceased parents. What was the deceased parent really like? What memories tell the young people more about their dead parent as a person and a parent? In what ways do young people resemble the parent in looks and attitudes, and in what ways do they differ? Talking about these matters allows young people and natural parent to accept the loss and move on. At the same time, the deceased parent does not become remembered as an all-perfect saint with whom no stepparent can compete.

Openly discussing these and many other issues helps stepfamilies in a number of ways. First, it makes members' private wishes, fears, and goals clear and concrete. The ideas can be heard and considered. Then members can decide whether and how to use those ideas or whether they will not properly fit the individual stepfamily. By talking openly, members understand each other better. They understand their frame of mind and goals for the family and can decide how to meet each others' needs.

Openly discussing issues in stepfamilies also tells members they belong. Hopes and fears about family life come out in the open. When members express themselves and others listen and think about the ideas, family members show each other respect and thoughtfulness. No one member will get what he or she wants every time, but at least everyone will understand each other better. Sometimes others want the same things and all can agree. At times, compromises result. All the time, members feel valued and appreciated parts of the stepfamily. Confusion and conflict lessen because misunderstanding becomes less likely. Members begin to know each other as individuals and build bonds based on mutual respect and trust.

*Conclusion*

For stepfamilies to succeed, family members must be able to accept many things.

They must accept the reality of the important relationships begun and nurtured in the first family. Absent parents and extended family matter very deeply to young people even after the divorce. If at all possible, children should be able to keep their closeness to their absent parents and relatives without feeling guilty. In successful stepfamilies, not all important family members live under the same roof.

Stepfamily members also need to accept change. New people enter their lives bringing new personalities, new needs, new ideas, and new ways of doing things. This means changes, and everyone must adjust. Some changes are as big as moving to a new place, a new house, with new people living with you, and a new school. Some changes are as small as finding another toothbrush in the bathroom holder. Change somtimes means giving up your comfortable, easy way so that someone else in the family can have his or her comfortable, easy way occasionally. Fairness to all is important. Flexibility by all is important, too. Stepfamily members also need to accept the way other family members really feel. There can be no "instant love," no "replacement parents," and no "loving all children just the same." Family members may want to think these things can happen, but expecting them can bring only hurt and disappointment. Relationships need the desire by both people to spend time together and opportunities to learn about each other. Liking and respect can grow slowly when given time and attention. Love may or may not develop. Stepfamilies can be happy and satisfying homes even if some members do not love each other, as long as they show patience, kindness, and respect for one another.

Finally, stepfamilies need to accept that they are a real family. They are not a first family, but they are a real family—or can be—with adults and children really caring about each other and helping each other grow as healthy and able persons as well as working together for the benefit of the whole group.

Coping with stepfamilies is easy if people can be flexible in their actions, open in their goodwill toward others, patient in their expectations for success, and willing to risk caring for others again.

# Bibliography

The Stepfamily Association of America, Inc., has available a large collection of books and pamphlets on the various aspects of creating a successful stepfamily, from the points of view of parents, stepparents, and children. Write to them at:

602 East Joppa Road
Baltimore, Maryland 21204

Capaldi, Frederick, and McRae, Barbara. *Stepfamilies. A Cooperative Responsibility.* New York: New Viewpoints/Vision Books, 1979.

Carter, Elizabeth A., and McGoldrick, Monica, eds. *The Family Life Cycle. A Framework for Family Therapy.* New York: Gardner Press, Inc., 1980.

Cherlin, Andrew. "Remarriage as an Incomplete Institution." *American Journal of Sociology. 84* (3) pp. 634-650.

Clingempeel, W. Glenn. "Quasi-Kin Relationships and Marital Quality in Stepfather Families." *Journal of Personality and Social Psychology,* 1981, *41* (5), pp. 890-901.

Duberman, Lucille. "Step-Kin Relationships." *Journal of Marraige and the Family*, May, 1973, pp. 283-292.

_____. *The Reconstituted Family.* (A Study of Remarried Couples and Their Children). Chicago: Nelson Hall, 1975.

Francke, Linda Bird. *Growing Up Divorced.* New York: Linden Press/Simon & Schuster, 1983.

Gardner, Richard A. *The Parents' Book About Divorce.* New York: Bantam, 1980.

Gelcer, Esther, "Mourning Is a Family Affair." *Family Process*, December 1983, *22*, pp. 501-516.

Hunt, Morton and Bernice. *The Divorce Experience.* New York: McGraw-Hill, 1977, pp. 43-45.

Jones, S. "Divorce and Remarriage: New Beginning, a New Set of Problems." *Journal of Divorce*, 1978, *2*, 217–227.

Kosinski, Frederick A., Jr. "Improving Relationships in Stepfamilies." *Elementary School Guidance and Counseling, 17* (3), February 1983, 200–207.

Maddox, Brenda. *The Half-Parent. Living With Other People's Children.* New York: M. Evans & Co., Inc., 1975.

Perkins, Terry F., and Kahan, James P. "An Empirical Comparison of Natural Father and Stepfather Family Systems." *Family Process*, June, 1979, *18*, pp. 175-183.

Prosen, Selina Sue, and Farmer, Jay H. "Understanding Stepfamilies: Issues and Implications for Counselors." *Personnel and Guidance Journal*, March 1982, pp. 393–397.

Roosevelt, R., and Lofas, J. *Living in Step.* New York: Stein and Day, 1976.

Rosenbaum, J. and V. *Stepparenting.* Carte Madera, California: Chandler & Sharp, 1977.

Stark, Elizabeth. "Friends Through It All." *Psychology Today, 20* (5), May, 1986, 54–60.

Teyber, Edward, and Hoffman, Charles D. "Missing Fathers." *Psychology Today, 21* (4), April, 1987, 36–39.

Visher, Emily B. and John S. *Stepfamilies: A Guide to Working with Stepparetns and Stepchildren.* New York: Brummer/Mazel, 1979.

Walker, Kenneth N., Rogers, Joy, and Messinger, Lillian. "Remarriage After Divorce: A Review." *Social Casework*, May, 1977, pp. 276–285.

Walker, Kenneth N., and Messinger, Lillian. "Remarriage After Divorce: Dissolution and Reconstruction of Family Boundaries. *Family Process*, 1979, *18*, pp. 185-192.

# Media Bibliography

"Act Two" (Stepparenting). 1987. 23 min. 16 mm. video. rental. Perennial Education, Inc., 930 Pitner Avenue, Evanston, Illinois 60202

"A Kid's Guide to Divorce". 1987. (includes aspects of living with stepfamilies). 4 full color filmstrips. 4 cassettes. guide. Mulberry Park, Inc., P.O. Box 4096, Dept. C105, Englewood, Colorado 80155

"And We Were Sad, Remember?" (Death) 1987. 23 min. 16 mm. video. rental. Perennial Education, Inc., 930 Pitner Avenue, Evanston, Illinois 60202

"Children of Divorce" 1987. Filmstrips-on-Video. Filmstrips Guidance Associates, Communications Park, Box 3000, Mt. Kisco, New York 10549-0900

"Divorce and Separation" 1987. Sound Filmstrips, Guidance Associates, Communications Park, Box 3000, Mt. Kisco, New York 10549-0900

"Divorce and Separation: Marriages in Trouble" 1987. Sound Filmstrips, Guidance Associates, Communications Park, Box 3000, Mt. Kisco, New York 10549-0900

*Divorce Happens to the Nicest Kids: A Self-Help Book for Kids and Adults.* Michael S. Prokop, author. 1986. hard cover. softback. audio cassette tape. Alegra House Publishers, P.O. Box 1443-A, Warren, Ohio 44482

"Don't You Love Me Anymore?" (no date given) 1987-88 catalog. (It's Not Fair, Can I Count on Anyone Again?, My Dad Lives in Springvale, Could it Happen to My Family?) 4 full color filmstrips. 4 cassettes. guide. Mulberry Park, Inc., P.O. Box 4096, Dept. C105, Englewood, Colorado 80155

*Kids' Divorce Workbook.* 1986. Alegra House Publishers, P.O. Box 1443-A, Warren, Ohio 44482

*New Beginnings. Skills for Single Parents and Stepfamily Parents.* Dr. Don Dinkmeyer, Dr. Gary D. McKay, and Dr. Joyce L. McKay. 1987. Papercover. Research Press, Box 3177, Dept. H, Champaign, Illinois 61821

"New Beginnings. Skills for Single Parents and Stepfamily Parents" 1987. Multi-Media Kit. Dr. Don Dinkmeyer, Dr. Gary D. McKay, and Dr. Joyce L. McKay. Leader's Manual, 4 audio cassettes, *New Beginnings* book. Research Press, Box 3177, Dept. H, Champaign, Illinois 61821

"No Fault Kids. A Focus on Kids With Divorced Parents." 27 min. video. purchase. rental. preview. 1987. leaders guide. blackline masters. United Learning, 6633 West Howard Street, Niles, Illinois 60648

"Single Parenting" 20 min. video. purchase. rental. preview. 1988. leaders guide. United Learning, 6633 West Howard Street, Niles, Illinois 60648

"Stepfamily Living: Myths and Realities." cassette tape, one hour. Elizabeth Einstein, Stepfamily Association of America, Inc., 602 E. Joppa Road, Baltimore, Maryland 21204

"The Stepfamily Journey." Cassette tape, one hour. Elizabeth Einstein, Stepfamily Association of America, Inc., 602 E. Joppa Road, Baltimore, Maryland 21204

"The Successful Family" 1983. 3 color sound filmstrips. (includes one stepfamily). Social Studies School Service, 10,000 Culver Blvd., Room 532, Culver City, California 90232-0802

# Index

**A**
abandonment, feeling of, 20-21, 45, 50
adolescents
  living in two families, 134-135, 156-157
  reaction to divorce, 29-33
  as sexual persons, 32, 121, 128-130, 138-139, 145
  in stepfamilies, 121-145
adoption, of stepchildren, 118-120
advice
  of grandparents, 81
  parental, 2, 30
  of stepparent, 94, 97, 104
AIDS epidemic, 155
alimony, 34, 35, 55, 96
anger
  at absent parent, 21, 25, 37, 41
  at death of parent, 6, 12
  of divorced parents, 35, 38, 66
  at divorcing parents, 16-17, 23, 31, 76, 121, 155
  familial, 14
  at gay parent, 156
  parental, 22, 38
  at remarrying parent, 11
  at stepparents, 10, 57-58, 64, 72
  of stepsibs, 107
appreciation
  of family members, 7
  by parent, 22, 71
  of stepfamily differences, 79
  of stepparent, 71, 86, 133

**B**
behavior
  with absent parent, 38

acceptable, 61
  parent's newlywed, 72
betrayal
  by absent parent, 121
  of deceased parent, 10
  of divorced parent, 22, 44, 45, 68, 87
bisexuality, 155
blame for divorce, children feeling, 18, 24, 33, 42

**C**
children
  and adoption by stepparent, 119
  feeling pushed aside, 71-72, 79, 109, 130
  feelings of, after divorce, 19-23
  in first family, 54
  and name for stepparent, 115
  regression of, 24
  of stepparent, 101-102
  and stepsibs, 106-107, 109
  telling about gay parent, 156
  used by ex-spouses, 66
  and visiting arrangements, 65
  visiting absent parent, 41
child support, 28, 34, 35, 39, 55, 65, 80, 96, 97, 157
closeness
  to at-home parent, 41, 50
  emotional, 45-46
  of family members, 7
  to natural parent, 62, 71, 74, 79, 87, 100, 155, 167
  of second family, 93, 104
comparisons, of stepparent, 10, 67, 68, 89

competition
  among stepsibs, 107-109
  teen/stepparent, 127-128, 139-140
compromise, in stepfamily, 53
confusion
  of children of divorce, 24, 30
  of different names, 115, 117
  about discipline, 100-101, 132
  of parental roles, 66-68
  about stepfamily life, 64, 98
  of two homes, 65, 156-157
control, feeling in, 76, 123-124
  seeking, 41
cooperation
  of divorced parents, 66, 157
  in stepfamily, 53, 58, 79, 93, 96, 102, 123, 131, 133

**D**

dating, parents', 43-49, 146
death
  ending first family, 1, 34, 75
  from illness, 4, 5-6
  of parent, 1-4
decision-making, 29, 35
  by divorced parents, 65
  by stepparents, 53, 97
  by teens, 126, 132
dependability, in stepfamily, 53
depression, 6
  of children, 76
  of divorced parent, 21, 35, 39
  of survivors, 12
difference
  of first and second families, 53-56, 59, 79, 90
  of last names, 117-118
  of stepsibs, 106-107
discipline
  agreement on, 102
  by noncustodical parent, 152, 158
  enforcing, 35, 43
  relaxing, 30, 33, 38
  resisting, 4, 29
  of stepchildren, 59-61, 64, 92-93, 99-101, 102-103, 111-112
  teens' attitude to, 132
divorce, 13-33, 34
  adjustment after, 82
  blame for, 82
  children's reactions to, 23-33
  ending first family, 1, 75
  of gay parent, 154
  joint custudy in, 82
  and remarriage, 7, 10-12, 49
  telling children about, 16-19, 24, 33, 35
drinking
  parental, 15
  teens', 124

**E**

emotions
  buried, 6
  holding back, 57, 64
  mixed, 27, 79-80
  negative, 57
  showing, 12
expectations
  realistic, 59
  of stepmother, 85-86
  of stepparent, 78-79, 83
  unreasonable, 57-58

**F**

failure, feelings of, 11, 35, 40, 44, 51, 56, 64, 70, 83, 87, 97, 118, 157
family
  breakup of, 35, 39, 82, 90
  first, 1, 45, 104, 120

loss of, 54, 61, 75-76, 87, 94, 152
reuniting, 20, 25, 26, 50, 75, 87, 93, 98, 110, 114, 147, 155
teens' ties with, 121
keeping apart, 69-71
ready-made, 52, 58
"real," 63-64, 83, 85, 86, 113, 118, 120, 131, 161, 168
single-parent, 1, 4, 5, 34-52, 71, 130
and grandparents, 80-82
favoritism, and stepsibs, 108, 111-112
fear
of becoming gay, 156
of divorce, 16-17, 18, 24, 27
of place in second family, 73, 124
stepmother's, 85
flexibility
in planning visits, 38, 152-153
in second family, 55, 69, 83, 88, 104, 168

## G
grandparents
children living with, 87
role of, in single-parent family, 80-82
grief
at death of parent, 2, 7
at divorce, 25
time for, 12, 76, 156
guidance
parental, 2, 33, 43
by stepparents, 97, 132
guilt feelings
at death of parent, 3, 6
at divorce, 17, 18, 22, 39
at remarriage, 10, 11
of stepparents, 56-57, 62, 97, 101
at taking sides, 22, 27, 28

## H
helplessness, feeling of, 28, 29
homes, double, 82
homosexuality, 154-155, 158
honesty, in stepfamily, 53, 62
household, help with, 7, 10, 34, 36, 50, 79, 95

## I
ideas, unrealistic, 56-64, 83, 88, 97
identity, teens building, 125-126, 145
illness, parent's, after divorce, 35
independence, teens', 3, 29-30, 42, 88, 112, 121, 130, 134
avoiding, 124-125

## J
jealousy
child's, of stepparent, 72, 123
stepmother's, 89
stepsibs', 107, 109
Johnson, Samuel, 50
joint custudy, 83

## L
letting go
of dead parent, 6
of first family, 76, 156
life-style, gay, 155-156
limits, behavioral, 23, 33, 35, 38
enforcing, 69, 97, 102
new, 121, 131, 132
setting, 77, 92, 99
testing, 100, 102, 131
loneliness
of child after divorce, 21
of single parent, 8, 35, 43

of stepsibs, 110
love
  freedom to, 5, 6
  equal for all children, 61-63, 83, 112, 168
  many forms of, 50
  instant, 56-58, 63-64, 75, 83, 86, 88, 104, 134, 158, 168
  money as proof of, 109
  parental, 2, 22, 33, 35, 43, 75
  of stepparent, 58, 59, 76, 96, 104, 115, 133
lover, parent's, 31, 32, 45-46, 51, 147
  hatred of, 48
  jealousy of, 47
lovers, gay parent's, 158

**M**
mealtimes, problems of, 89-91, 131
memories
  of deceased parent, 10, 12, 64
  of first family, 90
  parents avoiding, 21, 39
model
  family, 54-55, 63, 69, 133
  parents as, 4, 125, 126-127
  stepparent as, 128
money
  problems in stepfamily, 80
  and stepfather, 96
  and stepsibs, 109
mother, divorced
  absent, 88, 89
  closeness to, 98
  and income, 34
  "real," 85
  and son, 26
mourning, time for, 4-5, 6-7, 76
myth, wicked stepmother, 85, 92, 104

**N**
names, in stepfamily, 114-118, 160

**O**
obedience, 58, 60, 64, 76, 85, 88, 96, 102, 104, 115, 132, 134

**P**
parent
  absent, 1, 20-21, 24, 25, 59, 64-66, 75, 76-77, 79, 87, 97, 104, 110, 119
  and adoption, 119-120
  failure to visit, 147
  going to live with, 135-138
  additional, 59, 60, 76, 78, 88, 102, 104, 133, 160
  gay, 154-158
  idealizing, 7, 29
  instant, 58
  loss of, 57
  noncustodial, 152
  replacement, 8, 9, 52, 58-59, 63, 76, 78, 88, 102, 104, 134, 145, 168
  as sexual person, 31-32, 45-46, 138-139
  single, 1, 21, 98, 155
  surviving, 5, 7, 8, 9, 11
parenting
  by remarried mother, 100
  by stepparents, 59-60, 67, 86, 94, 95
  agreement on, 60-61, 100
  of teen, 133
patience, in stepfamily, 63, 75, 80, 153, 168
possessiveness, 4, 123
problems
  marital, 17, 35, 154

stepchildren's, 9, 12
stepmother's, 88-94
stepsiblings', 105-106
protection, parental, 2, 21, 24

**R**
rejection
 of absent parent, 42
 feelings of, 20-21, 22, 40, 41
relationship
 with absent parent, 39, 135, 157
 continuing, 1-2
 defined by names, 115-116
 emotional, 1, 9
 with gay parent, 156
 losing trust in, 6, 18, 57, 87, 121, 123
 new, 10, 13, 22, 42, 53, 74
 parent/child, 9, 10, 17, 20, 37
 romantic, 44-45, 49, 147
 with stepparent, 49, 68, 85, 88, 97-98, 102
 stepfamily, 54, 56, 62
 among stepsibs, 110-111
 teens', with friends, 131
remarriage, 23, 29, 32, 55
 and children, 49, 71-75, 111, 124-125
 after divorce, 11-12, 20
 new child in, 112-114
 planning for, 56
 reasons for, 49-52, 58
 after widowhood, 7, 8-10
respect
 love based on, 56
 for mother, 99
 in stepfamily, 58, 59, 60, 63, 69, 71, 96, 102, 115, 132-133, 168
responsibility
 children taking, 27-28, 29, 30, 32, 36, 122

divorced mother's, 34-35
divorced parents', 82
in first family, 54
of stepfather, 95
rivalry
 of stepsibs, 105, 108, 110
 teens/stepparents, 127-128
rules
 agreement on, 60, 102, 132-133
 enforcing, 97, 100, 133, 158
 fair, 111-112
 new, 121, 123, 131, 132, 145, 153
 relaxing, 38
 setting, 33, 35, 77, 92, 99
 testing, 102, 131

**S**
sadness
 of absent parent, 39
 of children of divorce, 20, 24, 25, 29, 76, 121, 155
 of stepsibs, 110
 of survivors, 12
security
 children's need for, 19, 30, 43, 75, 82, 155
 economic, 55
self-confidence, 18, 44, 51, 122, 126, 128, 134
 loss of, 81, 124
selfishness, parental, 31, 42
self, sense of, 29, 75, 121
self-worth
 loss of, 11, 21, 35, 41, 44
 regaining, 8
sensitivity, in stepfamily, 53, 151-152, 154
sex life
 of divorcing parents, 27, 31-32
 of single parents, 7, 44
 of stepparents, 53, 129

teens embarking upon, 128-129, 139
sexuality, in stepfamily, 139-145
shock
  of family breakup, 1, 33
  of remarriage, 49
stepchildren
  and mealtimes, 89-91
  resenting stepfather, 99
  and stepmother, 87
stepfather
  goals of, 97
  legal position of, 95-96
  and sexuality, 143-144
  types of, 94-95
stepmother
  reasons for marriage, 86-87
  types of, 84-85
stepparent
  gay, 157-158
  jealously of absent parent, 67
  living with, 84-104
  and sexual attraction, 140-141
  visiting, 1
stepsiblings
  living with, 105-120, 131
  and new child, 112-114
  and sexuality, 143-144
stress
  family, 14, 17, 30, 121
  marital, 14-15
  stepfamily, 75, 80
  with stepsibs, 107
support, emotional
  by grandparent, 81
  loss of, 7
  parents' need for, 26, 32, 44, 50, 51
  by stepparent, 42, 55, 67

T
taking sides
  by grandparents, 82
  between parents, 22, 23, 26, 27, 31
teasing, about gay parent, 154, 157
tensions
  family, 14, 15, 22, 30
  stepfamily, 64, 79, 83, 156
  of stepsibs, 107, 116
terror
  at absence of parent, 20, 24
  at death of parent, 2
tolerance, in stepfamily, 53, 55
trust
  betrayal of, 23
  growth of, 59, 60, 62, 64, 86, 102
  love based on, 56
  in parents, 17, 19, 33, 99
  loss of, 75, 150

U
understanding, in stepfamily, 53, 55, 59, 63, 75, 79, 80, 86, 133

V
violence, family, 14, 15-16, 27, 76
visiting
  absent parent, 37-43, 65-66, 70, 134-135, 156
  stepsibs, 106, 108, 109-110

W
wedding, first versus second, 52